SHANE EDWARD LEE

A GOOD BOOK

Shane Lee was born in Savannah, GA. He served in the United States navy, but was discharged after falling more than 30 feet. Since then, he has battled the Veterans Association to earn his due payments. A disabled veteran, he has taken to Youtube and has numerous subscribers. He is most famous for singing the Five Octaves.

Published by Lulu

First published 2011

10 7 4 2 1 5 9 6 3 8

Set in 11.5 and 10-point Crimson

A CIP catalogue record for this book is available

978-1-447-78698-6

www.youtube.com/user/shane12lee

For my parents, grandparents,
and God.

Contents

Humble beginnings

shane12lee   ⌄   Subscribe

▶ ◀))   0:01 / 3:22   380p ↗ ⤢

👍 Like ❓   + Add to ▾   Share 🏳   **130,059** views

Uploaded by shane12lee

0 likes, 0 dislikes

I guess you could call me nomadic.

We were like Jesus, Mary and Joseph, me, my mom and dad. The Bible tells us they wandered around an awful lot, from one home to another, and so the Lee family did too. Obviously, I don't know much about my childhood, given that I wasn't one of those people who was lucky enough to be granted a photographic memory, but like most kids I have incredibly vivid memories like Polaroid photographs that enlighten fleeting moments but leave the rest in the shade, all away from the flash of the camera.

I find it strange, how our brain is wired to commit some stuff to memory with the most perfect detail while others are discarded to linger in the half-light or leave our mind entirely. I suppose that those memories which you remember – even if they seem, looking back, to be totally unimportant – actually do have a significance beyond that which you initially see. Your mind wouldn't commit it to paper otherwise: it'd throw it in the trash, along with the majority of a person's history.

One thing seems to constantly run through all my memories of childhood that I can still recall today: my nose. It was always running. I had *everything* wrong with me as a child: colds, fever, chicken pox with the enormous blotchy spots on your skin, mumps and measles – you name it, I had it.

I had a cold when we went to Tybee Island – a place near my hometown of Savannah, GA, which has gone through a bunch of name changes. It was originally Tybee Island, then it became Savannah Beach because of its proximity to the city, then they changed it back to Tybee Island, though the two names are interchangeable really. It has a beautiful pier and a beach which runs for miles with golden sand on which the Atlantic laps: it's incredible today, and as a child, and with the halcyon memories filter that you always seem to have for childhood memories, it was even better back then. Today Tybee Island still take pride in their beach: there's an annual parade with huge floats that they call the Beach Bum parade, and the guys and girls on the float often get out supersoakers and drench the people watching the parade. They seem to like it though, because everyone's smiling and having fun.

Everyone was smiling and having fun in my childhood when I went to Tybee Island, too. Interesting fact: the Days Inn hotel chain started off in Tybee Island. Every time you go to one of those, if you're a travelling salesman, and you check in at their desk, just think that it came from my corner of Georgia. It might help you get off to sleep better.

Anyway, there I was at Tybee Island, playing in the sand, in the shadow of the huge, 250-year old Tybee lighthouse, which seemed even bigger when I was just a kid, and I have this horrible cold. My sinuses are killing me, my throat burns, and my nose is gunked up with all kinds of mucus. But I'm having fun, frolicking in the sand, looking up at my mom and dad and gathering pebbles and shells on the beach. The sun's breaking through the blue and white tower of the lighthouse, and I feel innocent and happy.

That was one of the good times.

I experienced a little bit of everything, both good and bad, growing up. I guess you could say that I had two competing powers on either shoulder: an angel to my right, looking after me, and a devil on my left, whispering evils and making bad things happen. They call it the sinister side for a reason, you know.

I'm telling you this, laying it all out in this autobiography, because I believe in complete honesty, and not hiding my mistakes, or making excuses, though I believe that we can be influenced, and get confused about things, and that religious leaders sometimes add to that confusion, because they are confused about things, and don't really understand Jesus' message, which isn't about overcoming your mistakes with Judgment, but overcoming them with Love.

I was born on November 3rd, 1969, in Savannah, GA. I'm therefore a Scorpio, which should tell you everything about me – thought I should point out now that I don't believe in signs of the zodiac, because they don't align well with my belief in Jesus.

Scorpios are often introverted singletons, who are loyal to a fault and passionate, as well as resourceful. Hopefully you'll see as I write a little about my life how those traits have come to affect me, and how I've managed to get to where I am today (bumps in the road of life and all) by using what God gave me.

We're also known for some negative traits, too: we're often suspicious, manipulative and jealous, and I can't deny that I answer those as well. Like I said, I believe in total honesty and laying it all out there for the reader: I'm not going to hide my mistakes or make excuses about things that have happened in the past, and I'm not going to gloss over the bad times and pretend that my life or I am perfect. I'm not, and my life hasn't been either. It's been difficult – fraught with difficulties – and it's something that I've learnt to adapt to, and to find strength in faith to help me find my path through this complicated forest we call life.

That forest has come out against me sometimes, like a really creepy forest, the likes of which you see in the Harry Potter films. I've had my fair share of Whomping Willows looking to attack me and derail my safe passage through.

My life has been neatly tracked by three near-death experiences which in some way have definitely affected my life, my outlook and my demeanor ever since. I think they can't help but do that, when you get so close to realizing your mortality and what's worth worrying about and what's not on this earth. The first flirtation with death I had happened when I was really young.

When I was just two I was eating a Jawbreaker candy. I loved those things, even then! They were just like dummies to me, helping me to stop crying and soothing me to sleep. The flavors and colors they came in really held me transfixed when I was a baby and I used to ask my mom for them all the time when we were out – and sometimes she'd let me have them from the grocery store. Of course, then I'd get all excited and eager to get the groceries through the checkout, get into the car and taste the Jawbreaker in the parking lot. I remember thinking that it was soothing, to have such a thing in my mouth; to tussle with it using my tongue, to try and wear it down to the point where I could eventually see it, feel it, getting smaller and smaller in my mouth. Those things could last me a week, I swear, and once you got to the end you felt a real sense of achievement, even then.

They were ideal candy for a baby: obviously then I was still only just teething properly, so I couldn't chew all that much, which made sucking the Jawbreakers really easy and truthfully the only thing I could do. The problem was on this day that I'd managed to break down the Jawbreaker to a smaller amount. The problem was that the size it had got to was just the size of my oesophagus.

That's right: it got trapped in my windpipe. I could feel the muscles in my throat contracting around it as I desperately tried to get the Jawbreaker out of the way. Whatever I did, my windpipe seemed to just be wrapping itself around the candy, getting stuck to it with the saliva and sugar like glue. It was a horrible feeling! Suddenly everything slowed down and became blurry: my eyes watered as an automatic reaction, but I wasn't crying. It was just my body reacting to the horror, to this foreign object impinging on it. I couldn't have cried if I wanted to: I was spluttering and wheezing, unable to pass air through my throat because this candy was stuck in the way. My mom realized that something was wrong, because I started making these guttural devil noises, like I was possessed. It must have been almost as horrible for her to see me in that state as it was for me: obviously, I was young, and babies when they're young don't know how to react to things. If you see a baby on an airplane, for example, they start crying when the plane takes off because the pressure builds up in their ears and gets painful. It's something strange which they've never encountered before, and they don't like it. They start crying, and their parents get upset because their child is in pain and discomfort, and there's nothing they can do. They – and every adult – knows that to get rid of the pain all you need to do is yawn. You yawn and the pressure stops.

But if you tell a two-year old to yawn, yawn like a lion, they don't know what to do. They're helpless.

My mom was screaming and hollering, panicking about how to get this Jawbreaker out of my mouth. She said that I began turning cold and my eyes closed, the tears rolling gently down my cheeks when I was lying on my back. Looking back on it, being horizontal on my back was probably the worst position I couldn't been in. She began getting flustered, and all I remember was seeing her running about, screaming this and that about how she needed help. She was calling out for ambulances, neighbors, my dad, everybody, but still I was there, choking, the life ebbing away from me, my mom fading away from me before my eyes as they closed. Eventually I stopped breathing, she said, and lay perfectly still. Then, there, she became even more panicked and screamed out, at the top of her lungs, "God! Help me!"

And would you know it, reader, that Jawbreaker ball of candy popped right out of my mouth.

Don't ask me to explain how or why: it was a miracle. 'Miraculous' is a word which we overuse in today's society: people make a miraculous recovery from a cold or the flu to be able to make a presentation at a business meeting. Politicians make miraculous recoveries from trailing several points behind in opinion polls to be the winner. They're not miracles. We've watered down the word. But this was truly a miracle.

My mom said that she was struck still by fear that she was going to lose her child, so she hadn't given me CPR or mouth-to-mouth resuscitation. She said she couldn't have, even if she'd thought of it. Her thoughts were too frazzled to conceive giving me CPR, and had she, she would've been too panicky to actually be able to move. All she could do was call out to the Lord, to shout "God help me!", and God heard. And God removed that Jawbreaker from my throat, and I could breathe again and I could smile again.

I'll never forget when my eyes opened once more, and there was my mom, crying – broken, really – thinking she had lost me. I'll never forget the tears of joy she cried when she saw the Jawbreaker roll along the floor, picking up dust and carpet hairs, and she saw me open my eyes and move and breathe once again. She held me so tight that I thought she was trying to squeeze another Jawbreaker out of me; that she was worried the thing was still lodged in there, that she couldn't believe her eyes.

I guess that's what miracles are though: events so miraculous, so beyond the pale that they beggar belief and you question what you're seeing. You tend to remember miracles. Like I said before, I believe your brain is hard-wired to commit to memory the stuff which changes you, the defining moments of your life. Cheating death for the first time, being blessed by the Lord and given a second chance, rolling back that Jawbreaker and putting air and life into my lungs once more...that was a defining moment. I remember those conscious moments – before I passed out and when the Jawbreaker moved and I could breathe once more – more vividly than almost everything else. It's not normal. It doesn't happen to normal people. That's not how it's meant to go. The happy outcome of that happens to basically no-one. I was blessed. I was lucky. It was a miracle.

There have been two other events which truly changed my life, both of which allowed me to cheat death and come closer to meeting my maker than anyone would want or should be allowed to do. One came 14 years later, just before my seventeenth birthday. The other happened on September 15, 1994 – my payday. I got paid in luck. Both of those I'll come back to later on, as I progress through my life story.

They say the events of a life maketh the man. I can't disagree. Those things that happen, they affect you in some little or big way. It can be a conscious change: for example, even though I was barely aware of my surroundings and knew little more than I was in danger when I was two years old, when I was old enough to know the world, and pieced together my remembrances with my mom's retelling of the story, I knew that I changed consciously. I accepted God as my savior: quite rightly, because until my mom called out to Him I was headed for the morgue.

I've since lived my life in a way that could not necessarily be called Christian – because sure, I've sinned – but I lead a life which is tinged with the belief in God and Jesus.

I've had the angel on my right shoulder and the devil on my left. Sometimes I've listened to the angel. Sometimes I've listened to the devil. You can't shake either. But they've always been there, and I've led my life in the belief that there is a higher power, and His power is unshakeable. I've done some bad things; I've sinned, that's true. But I hope for forgiveness. I've lived a life, constantly watched by these twin powers on my shoulder: the angel, dressed all in white, cherub-like, and the devil, always conniving to get me into trouble, nagging at me to push the boundaries, break the law and do the wrong thing. I've been swayed by him too many times, and I've been deaf to my guardian angel too many times too. But to err is human, said Alexander Pope, and he's true. I just hope that the often overlooked second part of that quotation is just as true: to forgive divine.

There are things which I need forgiveness for: minor infractions and major errors, both. I truly believe that by working through my errors in life and admitting them, I'll be able to be forgiven for them and the grief they have caused others. That's why

I'm writing this book, partly. For me, it's a way to demonstrate that I have done wrong unto others, and that I recognize that, and would like to put myself forward to be forgiven. For others, it's a way for them to learn about my life – because I seem to be of interest to a great number of people – and to learn about my positive and negative aspects (the latter of which the majority of internet trolls seem to focus on) and to appreciate me better as a person. Perhaps, too, people who read this will be able to learn life lessons from it, or to see themselves in me, and see their own errors in mine. Hopefully, as well, it will prevent others from making the same errors I have made, and might in its tales of how I have overcome adversity and shaken off the claws of death three times, demonstrate that there is a positivity in believing in God.

Isaiah wrote in the Bible a creed which I live my life through, which I base my Youtube videos on, and which I'm holding onto as an anchor throughout the writing of this book. In Isaiah 1:18 he writes "Come now, and let us reason together, saith the Lord: though your sins be as scarlet, they shall be as white as snow; though they be red like crimson, they shall be as wool."

I wrote to several television shows trying to put across my life story, in the hope that they'd let me work out my problems there, and provide me with the help and advice that so often comes on those shows, but no-one replied to my letters. That's partly why I've chosen to pen this book: it will act as a form of confession and therapy, a way to try and spread the word of God and demonstrate that he does good things for people. I truly believe I have been touched.

The shows I wrote to are all big institutions: Jimmy Kimmel Live is one of my favorites. I watched its first episode, and have seen how it has progressed and evolved from its original form, and in it I see a lot of myself, constantly adapting and evolving to life's hardships and the stones it throws as I go on my way. I also sent letters to the Tyra Banks Show, and Ellen, but neither of them replied. Obviously I understand that they are busy people, and they deal with an awful lot of inspirational stories which run the gamut of life similar to mine, with similar peaks and troughs, but they seemingly did not seem to be interested. I don't know whether they thought that my story was too unbelievable to be true – whether they took it to be a series of falsehoods, or embellished, or whether it was too extreme a transformation for them to cover. It could well be that the content matter was too graphic, too sinful and too complicated to put across on television. I sent details and copies of all the documentation needed as proof – medical records, birth certificates, newspaper clippings – to Oprah (back when she was still hosting her daily show) and Montel Williams. They didn't get back either. I emailed Dr. Phil, Jay Leno, David Letterman – they didn't reply too. I might've been a bit too real, a bit too serious, for Leno and Letterman. They tend to like the laughs. I sent out tens of emails to television companies and producers at the programs: the View, Live with Regis and Kelly, Tony Danza, Jane Pauley, 20/20, Primetime, and Ripley's Believe it or Not. I just wanted to put across my extraordinary story, but no-one was interested. Local television were also standoffish, which is strange: my story has an extraordinary ending, and looks at God in a wholly positive life. I don't know many people – if any – who have survived what I have, and have cheated death so many times. All I know is that I was looking for redemption, and a way to tell my story, and I was rebuffed. So I'm here writing this, as an attempt to spread the word of God and to give my fans a little back story to my life, so that they can better understand the person I am today, and see why I gravitated towards Youtube as a way to put my message across to the world. All I can do is point the way that the eternal spirit is showing me, and share it with the world. It's up to you whether you listen or not. But I know that whatever you do not only shapes the world of today, but the world of tomorrow, and the future beyond that. So in that vein, to fully understand the world I inhabit today, you need to look to my past.

Others say that you take after your parents, and they make you the person you are. I took after my parents in some ways but not in others. For example, my parents were typical of young adults in the late 1960s, early 1970s: they pushed boundaries which their parents would never have dared. They were part of the free love movement, and they enjoyed taking liberties with their bodies that other people wouldn't dream of. They weren't all that holy, I suppose, which makes it strange that I am. Perhaps it's a reaction to their free living, relatively atheist lifestyle that I am the way I am and believe in God. They were quite liberal, whereas I'm not so ambivalent about politics. They took risks, where perhaps I don't take as many.

My mom and dad used to listen to the rock groups around that time, and loved playing them on their record player. They'd have all the latest vinyls by the rock bands that were beginning to push the boundaries of music from something happy and playful into a more extreme, violent form. My dad's favorite band was Black Sabbath, who formed the same year that I was born, 1969. They were one of the major British bands who managed to break into America, and I know that they received some pretty violent backlash from parenting groups and people who thought that they were being sacrilegious and were proving to be bad examples to youths and adults alike in America. They were one of the main pioneers of heavy metal, and I suppose my dad was drawn to them because of their working class background and the fact that they were willing to fight out against the norms. In fact, his favorite song from the band was 'Black Sabbath', which not only has Satanic lyrics ("Satan's coming round the bend, people running because they're scared") but also is famous for its big riff, which uses the diminished fifth, which is pretty much a shortcut way of demonstrating the devil in music.

The diminished fifth had an effect on me: one of the memories I have is of hallucinating and imagining when listening to it blasting out of my dad's record players during a party he was holding that Satan was there in the room, spreading his wings, casting evil all over us. Mom and dad used to hold these parties every few weeks with their friends, where they'd all come around and play music and relax, and as was typical of the time they had drugs involved. Their friends – who were almost all parents – would bring over their children and they'd let us play into the small hours of the morning in another room while they sat and played their Black Sabbath, or Iron Man records at full volume in the living room. One of my abiding memories is playing games with the other kids while Ozzy Osbourne's voice, muffled by the thin walls of our house, came pounding into my ears. I could pretend that it didn't affect me, but it did. I didn't really like it.

Nor did I like the drug use. You could always tell when mom and dad and their circle of friends used marijuana at a party, because it would stink up the house with that sickly sweet smell and the grey fog of it would waft into our room, even though we kept the door firmly shut. Occasionally, if one of the other kids wanted a drink from the refrigerator, I would have to go into the sitting room through the haze, and past their wine bottles and them all gathered around the centre table where they'd be playing cards or a marble game, and I'd get a bit dizzy when I returned with my friend's Coke.

In fact, smoking of any kind is problematic to me. When I was three, I accidentally set fire to a bed at our house because I lucked upon the matchbox my parents used to light their joints and cigarettes. When you're a child, fire is the coolest thing that there is, and you long to play with it. Partly it's the fact that it's drummed into you when you're younger that you're not to play with matches. Partly it's just that it's an incredible event, which I think goes back to when we were unable (or at least found it difficult) to harness the power of fire. But there I was, playing with the matches, and I accidentally dropped one. I had managed to set the match alight, and I watched it burn – right down to my fingers. I reacted in the only way any human does when they get burnt: I dropped the match. It landed on the bed, and it set fire to it. Luckily my parents managed to rescue me and tamp out the fire before it burnt the entire house down.

I didn't like the concept of doing pot, but my step-brothers did. In fact, I think they saw my parents stoned, playing cards or Yahtzee with their friends, and decided that they enjoyed the mellow it gave them. So they did it, sometimes. I'm not sure I necessarily agree with it, but then again you have lots of people – from the White House to your very own neighbors down the street – who think that it effects people, and makes them crazy, and you have an almost equal number who do it anyway. At the same time I also noticed that unless they were doing other drugs like cocaine, or crack, that it didn't affect their behavior all that much and they did it until drug tests were required at work, which was most of my childhood, which wasn't too bad because it therefore didn't affect overly me. I just personally wouldn't do it: I'm mellow enough without it, and didn't like it when they or my parents would. For example, sometimes they'd do it in the car, hotboxing I think they call it, while we'd be driving down the freeway, and I would get car sick from it. In fact, that's all it did to me really whenever I tried it: it just made me sick, and I didn't like the feeling.

There was also the problem of my mom's friend, which is definitely why I shied away from drugs. Both my parents dabbled with drugs – as everybody did then – and they particularly liked marijuana. They were like most young adults then; they liked the Cheech and Chong stoner films, and they even bought a couple of their records to play when they were at home. I never properly did drugs myself, though, because my mom's friend (who used to do an awful lot of drugs) managed to ruin his life through using and abusing. He was friendly, outgoing and nice to us as kids when he used to come around sober. But when he was on drugs, he was like an animal. His eyes would become sunken, his skin would be pulled extra-tight over his body so you could see the veins, and his bones would protrude out from his skin, pressing hard so you could see them. He became thin, and wasted away. His drug taking got so bad that he was admitted to the hospital because he lost the feeling in one of his arms; it became withered and weak, and he couldn't use it. I don't know if it was a direct result of the drugs he used – whether he was injecting – or whether it was simply the toll it had on his muscles, but eventually his arm was wasting away on his body. It became a liability, the doctors said, when he was in hospital, and was poisoning the rest of his body. It was useless, and would kill him by releasing toxins into the parts of his body which still worked. He eventually had to have his arm removed at the hospital, and would walk around from then on with his shirts pinned up on one side to hide the stump which remained. The vision of this one-armed man, who was once such a friendly, normal person, coming over to our house regularly, scared me, and scared me off drugs. I found solace in the Bible; in Revelations 9:21, where John warns about the *pharmakia*. The word used in the Bible is 'sorceries', which I don't think has to do with natural supplements or the kinds of things you get at health food shops or holistic medicine practitioners, but synthetic ones. I even dislike being given prescription drugs, and I try to avoid them whenever I can, because they too have side effects which can cause more harm than good. I always take from that passage in Revelations one main message: don't rely totally upon drugs, either recreational or pharmaceutical, but instead also believe that God – the spirit, or breath of life within you – is able to heal as well. I believe in that because of the experiences I've had where I've cheated death and been nursed back to health by His grace. While I was in the hospital following my problems I've been treated with medicine, but as soon as I've been discharged I've turned away from synthetic solutions, and have relied on God to help me with the pain and discomfort.

It's not always been easy: some days I hurt so much that I want to grab the nearest bottle of pills to relieve the pain. Some days I'm better. The days that I feel better are the days that I know my faith in God is being rewarded: he's treating me for believing my alleviating my pain, if only for 24 hours.

My memories of my childhood – in fact, most of my memories – are pretty scattergun, which I apologize for. Events in this book might not necessarily be in the right order; they might not be as chronological as they should be. I'm not going to be able to lead you directly from my birth to the present day in a straight line, because my life has been anything but a simple path on the straight and narrow. I've deviated, I've erred. I've made my mistakes, and I've doubled back more than once. Sometimes I've seen something which has triggered off a memory in the past, and where that happens I'll digress in the story to tell you. You're getting my life, but my life through my eyes, with all the interlinked associations that a mind makes when considering your past. It's already happened in the section you've read so far: it took 700 words to get to my birth, where ordinarily my birth might be a natural place to start. That's simply the way the mind works: you associate one event with another, and you can't prevent yourself veering off into another story. It's the way we talk and the way we think as humans. When your life has been as extraordinary as mine, as packed with incident and intrigue as mine has, you have even more divergences to hamper your way. We've already begun our journey, with some explosive admissions. There'll be plenty more to come.

2009 was when the recession really hit me in adulthood. I'd known scrimping and saving as a kid, but like most people things had got better as I got older, and equally like most people, things fell apart around 2009. We had – and still have, despite all the economic turmoil we've undergone – a problem in this country. Paper costs maybe one cent a sheet. Someone is trying to sell it for five. That means the charge of four pennies in the five cent piece of paper – which, remember, only costs a single cent per sheet – goes to the cost of work. The four cents magically appear out of nowhere. We're overpaying for stuff. I've got this piece of paper; it's worth maybe a cent, but someone is trying to tell it to me for five. That means I have to come up with four more pennies than the piece of paper is actually worth. This country in which we live is only worth so much money, and the problem is that we're buying so much more than we're worth. We buy dollar shoes, or pens, or reams of paper, which cost five cents to make; that's a 95 cent profit which we don't have to pay – it's just disappearing out of our pockets, because we're paying too much for stuff. We're paying money for things which aren't worth that amount. It's a travesty, and it's what bankrupted this country. Not Wall Street. Main Street. Buyers paying over-the-odds for goods which have been overpriced from the cost it is to make them.

I agree with Walmart. They have a policy for their suppliers: if the product doesn't change year-on-year, then the price they're going to pay for the goods – the price they're going to charge their customers who shop there every week – has to drop. They're the largest grocery store in the world! The largest retailer in the world! They made $405 billion in sales in 2010, and they give their consumers 'every day low prices'. They say so, right on their advertising. A few years back, they sold an entire gallon jar of pickles for $2.97. $2.97! They cannot have been overcharging for that; there's barely a profit in it. If a pickle jar costs a certain amount, they say that they'll pay that amount and no more – and it has to be cheaper next year. That's the way we should live our lives, and the way we should spend our money. We should pay the real cost of things. If it only costs one cent for a piece of paper, we can't spend five. I'm not going to spend more money than something is actually worth. That's how we got into this mess.

We were a poor lower, or lower-middle class family growing up in Savannah in the early 1970s. Our Christmases were alright – I remember getting cool toys, and spending most of Christmas Day running around our house being excited at the concept of a whole set of new things to play with for another year. Our Thanksgivings, we took stock of what little we had, and we were thankful for it. We didn't complain or whinge; we just took what we were given and were grateful. We were careful with our grocery shopping, making sure that we paid the right price for food. I guess that's where I *do* take after my parents after all.

Our cuisine was the kind of stuff you get in houses all over Georgia that were in a similar situation to ours: honest, good southern cooking, with things like country fried steak with bell peppers, or crispy fried chicken and biscuits; pork chops with mashed potatoes, gravy and some sort of vegetable.

A lot of our vegetables were canned: they're cheaper, I suppose, and some of them can taste cruddy – especially then, when food preparation and quality wasn't so rigorous as it is today – but some of them were good. We had our own vegetables growing in the garden, which we tended to. We used to get great green beans from those. They weren't stringy, they were succulent and sweet and had just the right crunch. Nature's gifts can often be the best.

We were also lucky that our Granddaddy Lanky, who lived close by, had an enormous garden in his back yard which constantly seemed to be in bloom with one vegetable or another. As you moved through the seasons there would be corn, fresh on the cob, and golden butter beans bursting from their pods, plus snap peas which would be crisp between your teeth and cool on your tongue. Lanky also grew okra and squash, but I didn't like either. Squash tasted to me like it was just wood, and okra can quite easily be slimy. Likewise, I don't like, and never have liked, onions. I don't understand how, because most people seem to love the taste of them, and they're used in so many different styles of cooking, but for me they seem too pungent and powerful for my tastes.

We ate junk food, too: don't get me wrong. I still eat pizza and hamburgers, and used to love hot dogs with mustard and ketchup. Spaghetti I love – I even prefer the Chef Boyardee version that you can get in supermarkets to the home made kind, and their meatballs too.

Breakfast was always filling: that much my parents instilled in me. It sets you up for the day, a good breakfast, so they always made sure that it would give me enough energy to survive until lunch. We'd have cereal if it was a school day and we were in a rush to get the bus, but on weekends – or if mom had enough time – it would be a hearty breakfast of eggs and bacon. For a treat at weekends and public holidays we would be able to have French toast, which I always looked forward to.

Childhood was both brilliant and awful. I enjoyed being a kid, but I didn't enjoy how mean children can be. I had a few close friends, who were always supportive and friendly, but I was often picked on by both boys and girls, because I was a meek child. Unless you go out there and assert your authority when you're a child, you often get overlooked and picked on. The same is true as an adult, actually. The go-getters, even if they're not the smartest, or the fittest, or the best, always seem to end up on top. If you're brilliantly talented, but you don't have the courage to raise your voice beyond the crowd, to stand up and be counted, or to put your head above the parapet and risk getting shot down, you're unlikely to succeed as far as those who have boundless confidence. If there's one thing I could go back and do over, completely change, I mean, about my early years, it would be that I would be more confident in myself. You are your biggest supporter: only you know the boundless possibilities that you could have. If you're not going to shout about them, who is?

That's the way a lot of lives are, though: you have to try and look on the positive side of life, because you'll very often get a mixed bag. I said earlier that I used to love going to Tybee Island and playing in the sand. However, I also had a bad experience there, showing the combination of how things can be brilliant and awful (and hold bad and good memories) simultaneously in your mind.

I wasn't the steadiest of children when I was younger. I could fall over a fair bit, it's fair to say. On Savannah Beach, despite it being the home of so many happy memories, I had an accident. I was walking along the beach, picking at clams and winkles in the rock pools there, when I was really young and those sorts of things fascinate you because they're so unlike anything you know up to that point – they have *shells*, and *valves*, and they're *gray and slimy* – when I slipped on a rock and fell into a shallow pool of water.

A lot of people laugh when someone reels out the common trivia fact that you can drown in an inch-depth of water, but it's true. I know, because I did. It was awful. I slipped on that rock and fell face first into the pool of water, which wasn't at all deep but still suffocated me nonetheless. The water rushed up my nostrils and into my mouth: the pressure pressed against my eyeballs, and I could feel my sinuses throbbing as the blood pulsed through them. I gurgled; it was meant to be a scream for help, but was muffled by the water. I was fighting to right myself and to get back up, to escape the water; to escape drowning and death. I couldn't. I just could not turn myself the right way round. It was like I was an upturned, helpless turtle, except that my throat was clogging up with saltwater and I couldn't opening my eyes for the stinging sensation. I kept fighting and fighting, but I could feel my sense of fight ebbing away. All I had wanted to do was look at the limpets and clams and see their fluted shells, their hard homes which protected their soft bodies. Eventually, when I thought all my fight was gone, I felt a pair of familiar fingers clutch me around my waist: my mom. She had come and rescued me, saved me from what I thought was certain death. I spluttered and spit out unpalatable water as she raised me up and righted me. My face was drenched and my eyes were red, partly from my body reacting to the shock and partly because of the salt boring into them, working at the tear ducts.

There were a lot of mishaps which ran through my childhood, which I think is something that's shared by a lot of kids. Perhaps they don't find themselves in quite as much peril as I did (they might lose a tooth in a swimming pool, or graze a knee, rather than come close to dying) but there are still the same number of incidents.

When I was four I had a toy car. I loved that car. I'd race it around the room, around the sidewalk, around school, and it was the fastest car that there was. Evil Knivel would have loved to have driven this car: it would've given him the best stunt ride that was possible. It could reach 300 miles an hour, and it could leap canyons in a single bound. It was a Hot Wheels car, and any child worth his salt knows that Hot Wheels cars are the best. You only need to look at the television adverts to see that: they can loop-the-loop while most cars can only drive normally. Matchbox cars were good as well, because they were similar to the real cars that my mom and dad used to drive. I liked collecting Matchbox cars, but this car was a Hot Wheels, and it was bright orange, with go-faster stripes. It was my favorite, and this day it was about to try its hardest challenge; its most dangerous stunt.

I had a ramp set up over one of those cement breezeblocks with the two square holes in the middle. This was a giant factory, owned by the Hot Wheels corporation, which was sponsoring me, Shane Lee, world famous stunt driver, to try and jump over it. The holes in the middle were giant steel smelters (I don't know why, I was young and presumed that they would have such machinery in their car factory. Besides, I was young and fire and danger was cool), but I wasn't worried. My car could leap it all. It would power up the ramp, take off in flight and fly a smooth arc over the factory, landing safely on the other side. I'd done a trial run, speeding to the very end of the takeoff ramp, to see if I had got to the optimum speed. I stopped on the precipice of the ramp and let my imagination spot how the flight would go. It was perfect.

It came time for the actual stunt to go ahead. I would actually let go of the car, I decided, because that's what made it a stunt. The car would fly over the building of its own volition. I could get it up to speed and guide it on its run-up, but once it hit the ramp it was the car against gravity. I could feel the butterflies in my stomach. I imagined that I was putting on my fireproof undergarments, then my racing uniform and my helmet. I was getting strapped in to the car, testing the primitive rollcage by shaking it. I'd wave at a leggy blonde girl in the crowd and blow her a kiss. She would cry out of fear and nervousness at what she was about to see. I was off.

The car flew, reader, and it flew well. But the angle of the run-up wasn't quite right, the speed not quite enough. I watched the car plummet into the factory, into the cement block. I was devastated, because in my imagination I had just driven head-on into a burning hot smelter and horrified my audience. In reality I just had to pull the car out of the hole, and I could try again, my ego bruised but my body still intact.

The car was stuck. It would not move out of the breezeblock. Somehow it had gotten wedged in, and I couldn't get it out. I started to cry. This was my favorite car, and it seemed lost to eternity, stuck in this stupid concrete block. I remember my mom came in and asked why I was crying. I explained to her about the stunt, and how the car was stuck. She tried to get it loose, but couldn't. I told her to call the Fire Department to get them to get it out, but she said that was stupid, and they wouldn't come out for that. So reader, I put my hand in the block, and made it become stuck. It was really wedged in, alongside the car, and my mom could not detach me from it. I surprised myself with how easily and quite how well I had managed to jam my arm into the block. I'd only meant to threaten it, but I somehow became well and truly stuck. Then she *had* to call the Fire Department. I was going to get my favorite car back.

The firemen came and looked at me, and decided they had to crack open the block from around my hand and the car. My mom was worried, of course, but they assured her that if I kept extra still I would be okay. I knew that I had to keep still – not because I might get hurt if I moved (I wasn't worried about that), but because I wanted my car back. My fingers wrapped around it, and I held the car tight while they worked. It took a while, but they broke the block from around my hand, and I triumphantly raised the car up, joyous that I had made a full recovery from a death-defying stunt which had gone horribly wrong. They didn't understand; they laughed, of course, but I was proud. Looking back, I'm even prouder. This showed determination to hold onto something I wanted, or needed, and not to give up until I got it. It's something that I remember today, when I'm struggling against the world and problems. When I didn't get any replied from television shows about telling my story, I remembered my Hot Wheels car and the block, and took solace. When people leave hateful comments on my Youtube videos, I remember the car and the block, and realize that I want to spread the word of God – the real word of God – and that I'm tasked to do so. I won't give up. I'll never give up.

Most of my childhood was spent outside (something you'd expect, living in Georgia all of my life) so I'd get really deep suntans come early spring, which would last all the way through the summer. That changed when I hit puberty, though: before then, I would tan so much that I'd be thought of as an African-American when walking down the street and people would try and talk jive to me, which was shocking because I didn't understand what they were saying. When I became a teenager, I began staying in more and more, and my skin pigments changed resultantly. I'd often burn after a few hours in the sun after that.

When I used to tan really deep, I'd fit in okay with our few African-American friends. Georgia obviously has a long and troubled history with racism dating back to the Confederacy days, but I've never seen any racism from our family, or any slavery either. However since growing up, I've learnt that my great granddad was part of the Ku Klux Klan. I never knew that, and if I had I wouldn't have agreed with it, so me and that old man would've fought long and hard and had deep philosophical debates about the rights and wrongs of racism, with me convincing him that you have to love everyone equally. It's just strange to think that when I was younger he probably would've called me a little nigger boy because I was so dark myself. All that because I used to play outside lots and tanned easily. It's a shame that racism ever existed, really: it's wrong, totally and entirely. I don't think – or I'd like to not think – that my granddad agreed with my great granddaddy about race, but sadly for some people it's generational, and they can't countenance racial equality.

We moved about a lot: 'nomadic' was the word I used to describe it at the start of this book. We had a cat called Morris, named after the cat from the television, who got hit by a car. That was a bad, bad memory: I remember seeing him all messed up on the roadside, looking like death, his guts spilling out, for all the world looking like roadkill. But then (and this is where my memory might be confusing me, because though I have bright reminisces of some events others are kept in a fog of confusion) I remember us either finding another cat who looked exactly like him, or Morris managing to live, maybe resurrected by God for me. Either way he survived our first move, which was from our place off Victory Drive in Savannah, to the apartment me and my mom had in Garden City – Chatham City Apartments, the building was called.

I first started school at Skidaway, and used to like it, but hated being at home. The reason was that our next door neighbors had a kid who hated me. Truly hated me: for some reason, I repulsed him, and he made my life a living hell. We didn't move for that reason, though. We moved because me and my mom moved out and we couldn't afford to stay at Skidaway.

That was awkward. I couldn't understand at the time why we moved out; why my mom didn't love my dad anymore. They said they did, but I'm not so sure. I think that when divorcing parents say that they still love each other, they confuse and affect their children. It's better to admit that you don't love your partner anymore, than to lie for the sake of your child (who knows better anyway). It was actually my mom who divorced my dad: the whole episode was unpleasant, and it's at times like those that your extended family – the raft of aunts, uncles, cousins and grandparents – really come into their own. They tend to gather around you, like a protective shield, and ensure that the bad doesn't get in. Divorce is an ugly thing. People who are divorcing throw around insults and slanders at each other like there's no tomorrow, and they don't have a second's thought for the lasting effects on any children that remain in the relationship. If you have held your parents up to a certain model of virtue (as all children do), and you believe that you parents can do no wrong, and they know everything, then when you realize they're human after all it is crushing.

I thought my dad was superhuman before the divorce. I was six when they split up, and I thought my dad could do no wrong.

He was Batman, Superman and the Incredible Hulk all mixed into one. Little did I know until later that he was the latter of those three a little bit too much. He'd get green with envy, and begin smashing things; often it would be my mom who would end up in the way of his rage. So eventually, having been hit one too many times, and nearing her wits end, she had enough and took me and moved out. Looking back, I'm glad that she did that. He was making her unhappy – whether it was fuelled by the drugs they took and the music they listened to, I don't know, and I wouldn't want to cast aspersions – and it was for the best. We became, ironically, a more complete family when it was just me and my mom, and our extended family.

Our two-bedroom apartment off Victory Drive was near the Bacus Cadillac-Pontiac showroom and the Burger King, where my mom got a part-time job to pay our way. I didn't spend much time there, to be honest. Mom was working a lot, so I got shipped out to my grandma's, and my aunt's and uncle's house. I learned how to entertain myself there. It could be quite difficult, especially when your cousins are all out, and all that's left is their toys, and you're devoid of people your own age. You need to keep yourself happy and entertained, so I'd create fictional worlds and interesting imaginary characters when I got bored of playing with their old weeble-wobbles and Lincoln logs.

I need to confess something here. While I was at my Uncle Ronnie's, I really wanted a candy bar. I was so hungry, and I had that childhood fixation on eating some candy that you know will never go away but will eat away at you, gnawing until you sate it. But of course I was young, and we were poor, and going through the divorce, and I didn't have any pocket money. Uncle Ronnie kept a penny jar – a great big glass thing, filled to the brim with the pennies he would get from the supermarket and vending machines and everywhere. He'd come home and pop those pennies in a penny jar, until they eventually created dollars that he could cash at the bank. He must have had four or five hundred pennies in his jar – maybe more! – and I realized, *he won't miss 25 cents for a candy bar.* So I'm ashamed to say, I tried to steal some pennies from the penny jar. I only tried once (and I couldn't get it open) but I'm still ashamed regardless.

The few cousins I had didn't seem like enough, so I was lucky when my mom started dating again after the split from my dad that the guy she met had children who became my step-siblings. I was still so young then, only six or seven, that I could quickly make friends with them and soon enough it seemed like they were blood brothers and sisters, who had been there my whole life.

My family ballooned exponentially after the divorce: my mom met Big Roddy, who was a father figure to me while he and my mom were dating (something which became legally enshrined when they married and he became my step-dad), who had two boisterous sons, Little Roddy and Mark from his previous marriage. They were two friendly kids: outgoing and active, they took me under their wing as a brother and made me feel at home. That's the one thing I really believe is brilliant about children, especially when they're young: they tend to adapt to difficulties and strange situations and make the best. They don't have any worries about things which adults would. To them, leaving an old family and creating a new one with different people isn't strange or awkward. Children don't have the fear of social conventions that adults do, which can sometimes hold two disparate families like ours were from gelling well.

But we made it work, because we were kids, and eventually mom and Big Roddy (whose name was Roderick Crutchfield) came around to our way of thinking and it was normal. In fact, the two of them gave me a little sister called Renee not long after they got together, so I had two step-brothers and a sister from my mom's new relationship. It was a big difference from being an only child as I was when my biological mom and dad were together.

I still saw my dad, too, until he died, and he managed to find happiness with another woman which only further increased the names on my Christmas card list. My dad met a woman called Myra, who was perfectly pleasant to me as a step-mom, and the two of them had a daughter called Shonda, who became my step-sister. Shonda was friendly, too, though because she was a girl I didn't get on as well with her as I did my mom's step-sons because obviously at that age the last thing a boy wants to do is hang out with a smelly prissy girl. Years later, when I was much older, they had a son called Little Bobbie. There was quite an age gap between Little Bobbie and me, though we still got along well whenever I went over to my dad and Myra's house.

Back before my mom and dad got divorced and had their own lives with different people, back when it was just the three of us, as tight knit as could be, we went to Disney World in Florida, making the short drive south across the state line to go to Orlando. I must have been about four or five, and I remember being so excited that I ended up just jumping up and down in our sitting room. I wanted to see Mickey and Minnie Mouse for real, having seen them in countless cartoons on Saturday morning television. The whole concept blew my mind, that you could visit Mickey and Minnie at their house! Though I always questioned why families would go to either Disney World or Disneyland without fully knowing Mickey and Minnie's movements. I mean, obviously everyone knows that Mickey and Minnie originally lived in Disneyland, and that Disney World is their summer vacation house! You'd want to time it so you went to the right place at the right time!

I really enjoyed Disney World, being amazed at seeing Mickey and Minnie up close. Primarily I was relieved that we'd come when they were taking their summer vacation in Florida, to be honest. But though I could handle rides like the Haunted Mansion, I definitely did not like the 20,000 Leagues Under the Sea ride. Perhaps it was something to do with me almost drowning, perhaps it was the creatures that they showed, or perhaps I wasn't feeling well that day, but I distinctly remember being scared when we got on and wanting to get off. When we went back to Disney World, when I was older – probably about 11 – I still skirted around that ride when we were in the Magic Kingdom. Disney World was our Mecca: we only went there as a special treat. I can't imagine what people who grew up in Florida, in and around Orlando, did for a treat when they had the most magical place on earth right on their doorstep. It seems to me like you'd be spoilt, or that the illusion of Disney being a brilliant place would be spoilt – one of the two must surely be the case. If we were good, though, me and my step-brothers and sisters, we would be allowed to go to Six Flags in Georgia as a more regular treat.

Six Flags is good, but it's no Disney World. It's not immersive: it's just a bunch of (admittedly wilder) rides gathered together in the same place without rhyme or reason. I can't complain – I liked the rides, and I liked the visits to Six Flags – but it didn't hold the same excitement as going to visit Mickey and Minnie down south in Florida.

I always remember the radio constantly being on when I was growing up, which I guess is natural when your parents like music as much as mine did. I think it explains why I tend to gravitate towards singing versions of songs so much for people on Youtube today. I'd always quietly sing along to songs that were played on the radio when I was a child, and because everyone sounds different when they sing a song (for example, Tina Turner sounds entirely different to Lady Gaga), and because no-one told me differently, I presumed that you had to mimic the person's voice whose song it was when you sung it. In fifth grade I was told to sing 'Georgia' by Ray Charles for an assembly we had, and I sung it just like I was Ray Charles. One of my schoolmates also did it, but he sung in his own voice and taught me that you can sometimes sing in your own natural voice, rather than trying to sound like the person whose songs you're singing. The thing is though, mimicking a singing voice proved better in the long run, because it's a large part of my Youtube cadre, and it has also helped me understand how to sing harmoniously with other people. It was a big help, for example, when I was in choir at school, because when you mimic a singing style for a song, you're trying as best as you can to harmonize with the original track. That's not all that different to what you do as a choir: individually, you try and alter your voice – mediate it, perhaps – so that it becomes as close to everyone else's voice as possible. If you do that well, you end up with a strong, individual tone for the entire choir. You don't want everyone in a choir singing off their own hymn sheet, in their own key: it wouldn't sound right.

I devoured books when I was younger, using them as a springboard for my own imagination. It's why I'm so pleased to be able to write this now; the concept of having my own book is something which astounds me, given that they were such a big part of my life growing up. I joined the book clubs at each school I went to, and ordered any and every book I could through it. I even ordered one that dealt with vampirism – the real one, not Dracula (though I read that too and got scared by it). I learned about Vlad the Impaler from this book, and other vampires like him who had actually taken the make believe out into the real world, but just like when I read and responded to 'A Clockwork Orange', I knew that even if you *could* do these things, if you're of a sane disposition you wouldn't. Those who were of a slightly more unhinged stance likewise shouldn't be able to do those sorts of things. If you're being influenced by the devil, that's your choice, and you're able (however hard it might be) to stop listening to his evil thoughts and ideas and control yourself. For example: I ordered a book that dealt with sex through the school book club when I was about 14. I read it to learn what to do with a woman when I was married. It taught me how to perform cunnilingus and different techniques to approach sex, but I was willing at the time to wait until marriage to have sex with someone. I was seeking knowledge, not a reason to act.

I was picked on at school, as the vast majority of kids are. If you're not in the fifth percentile of cool kids, or jocks, or you don't play the right kind of music or say the right kind of things, then you're bound to be picked on at some point or another. It's a sad fact but it's true. I'm not sure whether the ways I was picked on were routine or out of the ordinary, but they were numerous throughout the years. It didn't help that I was held back in the third grade: if you're held back, you tend to lose a lot of your friends and have to make new ones. Integrating into an established classroom of people, with their friends and friendship cliques, can be really difficult. I had a close friend, called Myron, who I met in the fifth grade. He was the one person who I really thought I could trust, and he stayed my friend for an awfully long time, even beyond us reaching adulthood. We would skip school during the daytime, and sneak out at night to explore when we were young and once we got older, to hang around the town and drive. At first we rode bikes, then we used his red 1963 Chevy truck to ride around town. For the most part, though, kids at school weren't all that welcoming. Once, a black boy made me prove to him that I was a boy. It was very strange. We were going for a bathroom break, and once everyone else left and it was just me and him in the bathroom he trapped me in there, and refused to let me out until I showed him my penis. I eventually had to show him my penis, prove that I was a boy, and he let me go. A little black girl also used to show me her underwear, all innocent like, which was confusing. In second grade we were watching the movie Peter and the Wolf in class. I don't know why – I think the teacher was bored of us, and put on this movie. It puts pictures to Prokofiev's composition, and it's really impressive to watch today. I enjoyed it back then too. I remember distinctly rolling about on the carpet in tears of laughter. I was young, and I knew that I was laughing so hard that I would eventually need to pee. I had a problem though: I was enjoying the movie so much that I didn't want to miss a single second by going to the bathroom, and the teacher was not going to stop the movie just for me – I knew that. So I did what any self-respecting child would do, and I just let it go. I started peeing right there in the classroom, while Prokofiev played me out.

The second time I took third grade I was better, scholastically. I really enjoyed it, I think because of my teacher. He was called Mr. Martin, and he took a shine to me and realized that he needed to let me express myself. I think he recognized that it was a frustrating place to be in, having to resit your third year while all your friends have moved up a grade, and he let me be me. Mr. Martin was great like that. He got us TV coverage on WTOC Channel 11, and we were interviewed by the local news guy for it, and he also let us perform a show for the entire school! I was nervous waiting in the wings, but I toughed it up and went out there doing voices, like Speedy Gonzales and the Incredible Hulk.

I was a big fan of comic books, and the heroes that were written and drawn about in them. The Incredible Hulk was cool, as was Batman, but my favorite was definitely Spiderman. Once I even tried to cut my hair like Peter Parker's, using a pair of rusty, blunt scissors that we had in the house. I was sat there, cross-legged on my bed, a mirror in front of me and a copy of the Spiderman comic at my side, flicking my eyes from the comic book to the mirror to try and emulate the hair style. It didn't quite work out. All I got was a bad haircut.

People can be so cruel, especially kids, when they don't know any better. On the school bus one day not long after I performed in our school show, doing my voices, a boy began picking on me. He'd say that I was gay, and tease me for it. I wasn't gay – though I didn't really know what it meant then, if I'm telling the truth – but he was insistent that I was gay and would tell everyone at the bus, trying to get them to join in the bullying and laughter. He said that it was in my eyes, the gay feeling. I had – and always have had – a problem with my eyes. I suffer from astigmatism, which causes my vision to be blurry and does, on the surface, affect the outward appearance of my eye. I have to hold my eyelids in a different way to most people to try and focus on what I'm looking at: my eyeball can't do the right job of focussing on objects, so I have to use the rest of my eye, including my eyelids, to try and improve its focus. Sometimes, because of the astigmatism, I blink uncontrollably. People get freaked out by it, but I can't help it: it just happens. It doesn't mean that I'm gay, as this boy thought (it's probably a thought that was put in his mind by a careless, throwaway comment made by his dad), it means that I have difficulty seeing. I still got picked on, gay or not, for that and many other reasons. Eventually I got surgery on my eye when I was about 12, which corrected my crossed eyes but did eventually weaken my eyesight in the long run. I don't wear glasses all that often, even though I find it difficult to see, because I can still see alright without them and besides, they distract me from the art of actually seeing anyway.

My eyes were metaphorically opened, however, when I was just over a month away from my tenth birthday, when an enormous storm came into my life, blew everything around and left it in tatters. The year was 1979.

Hurricane David was one of the worst hurricanes to hit land in the second half of the 20th century. It did more than one and a half billion dollars worth of damage, all told, at 1979 prices, and directly killed more than 2,000 people. I was enthralled and appalled David and the way it had ripped through countless islands before hitting land on the eastern seaboard and tearing its way through countless states, including Georgia.

It was my first hurricane, and it was foreboding something much worse which would come soon.

It hit us at the start of September 1979, and we were just a handful of the 400,000 on the eastern seaboard who were evacuated because of the threat of its powerful winds. Our evacuation was small-scale: we only moved from our house to my Aunt Jeanan's further inland, but it was still a big deal for a not-yet-10-year-old who was experiencing his first ever hurricane. I prayed and imagined that there was a protective bubble around that trailer we moved into every night, because I was scared. I'd been hearing about the devastation David had wreaked on successive areas, and I desperately didn't want to be another one of his victims. In the end we scraped through unharmed, but much worse was about to happen a few weeks later.

My dad's – my birth dad's – full name was Bobbie Edward Lee. He was at home with his then-wife, while I was out shopping at Redmonds, which is a clothing store. I was looking for some new slacks. It was midmorning.

A friend of my dad's dropped by his house to visit, the police said later. I don't know whether they were connected by the drugs which my dad was still using or not – I'm not sure I really ever want to know. At first, the conversation seemed amiable between him, my dad and his wife. They were chatting away about life, when suddenly it changed. He began shouting at my stepmom, then tried to hit her. My dad stepped in, as you would, and pushed him out of the door. My dad didn't know that his supposed friend had a gun on him. In the heat of the moment, this friend pulled the gun on my dad. He shot him. He shot him at close range. He shot him in the right cheek – just under the eye – and I tried not to cry about it when I heard, but it was hard. He shot him. I don't remember if the guy ran, or if he stayed, but he was soon arrested.

They were playing music on the radio at Redmonds when I was shopping for my slacks. I was walking down the aisle when one song finished, and the news guy came on the radio. He announced there had been a shooting in an area near where my dad lived. He said there had been a murder. And he said my dad's name. I tried not to cry about it, but I did. I broke down there in Redmonds.

It was the only time I cried about it.

I didn't even cry at the funeral. It was a shock, hearing it the way I did. I wasn't prepared. When I was prepared, when I'd managed to steel myself to the knowledge, I was sad but serene. I didn't cry then. But that was the moment that I truly began to follow my faith the most: it gave me the impetus to give myself up entirely to God, and to try and spread His word.

I had been part of the church – Rincon Baptist Temple – for a while, but I had been like most kids: I saw it primarily as a social event. It was a way to get together with friends on a Sunday, and to learn a few things was not really the primary objective. It was more a youth group than a religious following. However when my dad died, I began praying. I turned to religion to help me figure out why one of my father's friends could end up killing him when he had just dropped by. I wanted to try and explain what was at the time the unexplainable. I turned to God.

It took me two years to fully accept religion. I was baptized on November 1, 1981, at the church. In the run-up to my baptism I prepared myself for what was to come. I committed myself heart and soul to what I had learned about baptism in a pamphlet I was given, and knew from that flimsy piece of paper that this was my salvation and my calling in life. I requested the baptism myself, of my own accord. No-one else explained it to me. I rationalized that if I got baptized, I would be resurrected one day, like Jesus was. If I tried my very best to follow God, and live as good a life as I could by following Jesus and the Holy Ghost, I'd be saved. I'd been part of the church before then, going to Sunday school and on a few summer camps with them.

They were both good and bad. My friend Myron was there at the camps, too. We did everything together, and that included going to church. He helped me get through the shock of my dad dying; by his own admission, he didn't do much but be there, but sometimes that's all that you want. Adults like to try and improve things by actively making it better. They purposefully go up to a grieving person and try and take their minds off things in a most unnatural way. They'll propose going to the cinema when they've never before taken an interest in movies; they'll suddenly love golf, or baseball, or music. It's a sham. You can see through it entirely. Kids don't do that. They simply continue doing what they do, without drawing attention to the fact that they're helping. Myron did that. When he heard that my dad died, he simply did what he always did: he came over with the latest Spiderman comic book and a couple of toys, and we hung out and played. That was the most comforting thing anyone could do when I was faced by the reality that I didn't have a dad anymore. I sometimes wonder if he realized how helpful he was to me back then. He came with me to the summer camps the church put on, and we were both really excited by them.

The first camp after my dad died was in Florida, just about half a year later. I cried then. I had my first crush on a girl at that camp. Our eyes met over the campfire while we were singing 'This Little Light of Mine'; we both swam together in a creek; and we kissed. I was really happy not that long after feeling immense sadness. However the girl (I won't mention her name) broke up with me, and broke my heart, and suddenly I was upset and sad again. I cried out to God at camp, asking him to help me find the right woman some day. I hope that he is still up there and remembers my request, and does so during my lifetime. We went to another summer camp where a few of the boys had a bad experience.

One of the boys there came into our lodge one day and said that he had been almost molested by one of the camp counselors. We were shocked, and began telling people, and were all rounded up together and told to keep it quiet in exchange for preferential treatment. Our camp became a whole lot better because of that. A similar sort of thing happened to me when I went to the Christian Fellowship Church; the then-General Pastor hugged me in a back room and put his arm between my butt cheeks, down to the hole. He squeezed me tight and told me I was uncomfortable with my sexuality while stroking my hair. I've never told anything about this to anyone until now. I'm willing to forgive the pastor for what he did though, because I realize that like David and Bathsheba, the reason the Lord reveals the sins of people is so that we can, as a group, learn from them and not make the same mistakes.

The gray-haired pastor made a mistake and was a little too forceful with me. I dreamed during boot camp that a white-haired man kept trying to force himself on me, and it scared me a little. But these things are sent to try us.

That self-same pastor also counseled me on sexual matters. He told me that it was okay to masturbate and that Jesus allowed it, which at the time – as a young man who was beginning to feel sexual urges – I was surprised at. But I took to my books and specifically to the Bible, and I found a scripture which backed up his point. It was there, right in front of my eyes, in Leviticus 15:

> [1]And the LORD spake unto Moses and to Aaron, saying,
>
> [2]Speak unto the children of Israel, and say unto them, When any man hath a running issue out of his flesh, because of his issue he is unclean.
>
> [3]And this shall be his uncleanness in his issue: whether his flesh run with his issue, or his flesh be stopped from his issue, it is his uncleanness.

[4]Every bed, whereon he lieth that hath the issue, is unclean: and every thing, whereon he sitteth, shall be unclean.

[5]And whosoever toucheth his bed shall wash his clothes, and bathe himself in water, and be unclean until the even.

[6]And he that sitteth on any thing whereon he sat that hath the issue shall wash his clothes, and bathe himself in water, and be unclean until the even.

[7]And he that toucheth the flesh of him that hath the issue shall wash his clothes, and bathe himself in water, and be unclean until the even.

[8]And if he that hath the issue spit upon him that is clean; then he shall wash his clothes, and bathe himself in water, and be unclean until the even.

[9]And what saddle soever he rideth upon that hath the issue shall be unclean.

[10]And whosoever toucheth any thing that was under him shall be unclean until the even: and he that beareth any of those things shall wash his clothes, and bathe himself in water, and be unclean until the even.

[11]And whomsoever he toucheth that hath the issue, and hath not rinsed his hands in water, he shall wash his clothes, and bathe himself in water, and be unclean until the even.

[12]And the vessel of earth, that he toucheth which hath the issue, shall be broken: and every vessel of wood shall be rinsed in water.

[13]And when he that hath an issue is cleansed of his issue; then he shall number to himself seven days for his cleansing, and wash his clothes, and

bathe his flesh in running water, and shall be clean.

[14]And on the eighth day he shall take to him two turtledoves, or two young pigeons, and come before the LORD unto the door of the tabernacle of the congregation, and give them unto the priest:

[15]And the priest shall offer them, the one for a sin offering, and the other for a burnt offering; and the priest shall make an atonement for him before the LORD for his issue.

[16]And if any man's seed of copulation go out from him, then he shall wash all his flesh in water, and be unclean until the even.

[17]And every garment, and every skin, whereon is the seed of copulation, shall be washed with water, and be unclean until the even.

[18]The woman also with whom man shall lie with seed of copulation, they shall both bathe themselves in water, and be unclean until the even.

[19]And if a woman have an issue, and her issue in her flesh be blood, she shall be put apart seven days: and whosoever toucheth her shall be unclean until the even.

[20]And every thing that she lieth upon in her separation shall be unclean: every thing also that she sitteth upon shall be unclean.

[21]And whosoever toucheth her bed shall wash his clothes, and bathe himself in water, and be unclean until the even.

[22]And whosoever toucheth any thing that she sat upon shall wash his clothes, and bathe himself in water, and be unclean until the even.

[23]And if it be on her bed, or on any thing whereon she sitteth, when he toucheth it, he shall be unclean until the even.

[24]And if any man lie with her at all, and her flowers be upon him, he shall be unclean seven days; and all the bed whereon he lieth shall be unclean.

[25]And if a woman have an issue of her blood many days out of the time of her separation, or if it run beyond the time of her separation; all the days of the issue of her uncleanness shall be as the days of her separation: she shall be unclean.

[26]Every bed whereon she lieth all the days of her issue shall be unto her as the bed of her separation: and whatsoever she sitteth upon shall be unclean, as the uncleanness of her separation.

[27]And whosoever toucheth those things shall be unclean, and shall wash his clothes, and bathe himself in water, and be unclean until the even.

[28]But if she be cleansed of her issue, then she shall number to herself seven days, and after that she shall be clean.

[29]And on the eighth day she shall take unto her two turtles, or two young pigeons, and bring them unto the priest, to the door of the tabernacle of the congregation.

[30]And the priest shall offer the one for a sin offering, and the other for a burnt offering; and the priest shall make an atonement for her before the LORD for the issue of her uncleanness.

[31]Thus shall ye separate the children of Israel from their uncleanness; that they die not in their

uncleanness, when they defile my tabernacle that is among them.

³²This is the law of him that hath an issue, and of him whose seed goeth from him, and is defiled therewith;

³³And of her that is sick of her flowers, and of him that hath an issue, of the man, and of the woman, and of him that lieth with her that is unclean.

I don't know about you, but I've spent a large part of my life reading and interpreting the Bible, trying to make sense of them in this modern, complex world. This is my reading of this particular passage.

When it comes to sexual things, a man can have sex with his wife. That much is given, as long as she is willing. If she isn't willing, then he can't well go and rape her – that much is obvious, too. If she isn't willing, he is then to masturbate, according to Leviticus 15:17-18, while thinking of his wife – and only his wife! But if the man is unmarried, he may only think of a single woman. Here is where it gets complicated. If you are single, I take it as read that you can think of a married woman while masturbating, as long as you do so in the spirit of confession. As long as you don't commit adultery, God will help you out until you find your own wife.

If you read the passage quoted above, the man who spills his seed on his garment or skin (or on any garment, any skin, or leather) is simply to wash all his flesh in water, and be unclean until evening. However, if he sleeps with a woman they both have to wash (in the original text which I've pored over, masculine nouns have a *uw*, or *vav* at the end of them, or *iym* for the plural, though sometimes even verbs can have a masculine, or feminine ending) and be unclean until the evening. Now, I don't know about you, but to my mind there is only one way for a man to get his own seed of copulation on his skin or garment, and that is through masturbation. It's a private act, and it's perfectly acceptable in my reading, guided by the former pastor. If you want a sex doll (or something like that – a masturbatory aid, basically), then so long as you don't allow it to replace a woman, and are willing to rescind it when you're married, that is acceptable to Jesus.

I have regularly asked Jesus about these things, and get my answers through the scriptures. This definition of the scripture covers wet dreams, and sex where you pretend that your pillow is a woman (or a man for you ladies), because you are perfectly entitled to masturbate until marriage. Why else would Mosheh mention the passing of semen before sex with a woman? When you're growing up, which are you most likely to do first: masturbate or have sex? I know which the case was for me. You are, of course, going to masturbate first, and then have sex when you get married, so if done with respect towards marriage, and in trying to find one woman to marry you, God has in the Old Testament made allowances for it. To any parents reading this I would say that there is nothing wrong with this type of behavior. Don't try to embarrass your child or teenager! It is safer for them to masturbate even if it feels real than to have premarital sex in this day and age, because Mosheh said what he said in times of slavery, than to actually have promiscuous sex, and possibly get pregnant or contract an STD.

Until I realized this I had thought about being a eunuch for the Kingdom of God's sake. The pastor then opened my eyes to a world of sexual possibility by permitting masturbation; another pastor later told me it was alright for two grown men to masturbate together, so long as they aren't gay.

I was technically a virgin until the age of 21. Don't get me wrong: I fooled around a little with my girlfriends before then. One of them used to bring me incredible close. Lisa was my girlfriend when I was 16. We almost had sex; we would dry hump and rub together on the outside, but never have penetrative sex. Whenever she said stop, we stopped, and if I had to finish off I would go to the bathroom, out of respect for her, and do so.

Then when I was 19, I almost had sex again. The girl was 12, but wasn't a virgin. I didn't force anything; she was going from one guy to another, and had been regularly sleeping with someone in their 20s when I first met her. She even slept with my younger friend at my own birthday party, which didn't affect me in the least. I was about to stick it in her when she said "that's not it", so I stopped and nothing else was said. There was another girl, when I went out to Effingham, who used to like me. At the time I was always being picked on for being gay, so one night at a dance, I was tired of it and wanted to just have sex with her. Her name was Susan, but this night she could tell that I wasn't being my usual Christian self, and told me that she wanted to as well, but could tell that I wasn't being myself and wouldn't be doing it for the right reasons. I realized then that you don't have sex with a woman just to prove that you're not gay either, because a woman has feelings and doesn't deserve to be used.

Before I joined the navy I also had an old high school girlfriend who wanted to sleep with me before I left. She invited me over and was on the floor without any underwear on, and I was hard, but felt wrong about it, so I stopped. I was quick to let her know that it wasn't her, but that I was trying to wait for marriage as well, and believed that I was worthy of waiting, rather than wasting my virginity on a goodbye just days before leaving for service.

So up until the age of 21 I released all my sexual frustration through masturbation. Some might point out that Matthew 5:27-28 ("Ye have heard that it was said by them of old time, Thou shalt not commit adultery: But I say unto you, That whosoever looketh on a woman to lust after her hath committed adultery with her already in his heart") forbids masturbation, but masturbation isn't lust. There were times that other parishioners approached me sexually, but I did not give in to the temptation, because it was awkward and felt wrong. One tried to take a shower with me, but I fended him off; the other woke me up in the middle of a wet dream and wanted to masturbate with me, but I refused. I don't blame the individual parishioners, but the particular pastor for planting those ideas in their heads.

I even walked in on a parishioner molesting a little girl once. It was in the church, and I opened the door to get something and saw him there fondling her. He stopped as soon as I walked in and never did it again. I didn't know what to do or who to tell, so in the end I kept it to myself until now. The man did seem to understand that it was wrong to do so, and seemed to be shaken up about it (though undoubtedly nowhere near as shaken up as the girl he attacked). Eventually he married someone else, because he must have known that it is better to marry than it is to burn.

I believe that these events all built up to a crescendo which eventually caused a climax in my life. A lot of bad things happened to me, one after another, in a short period of time. I underwent tremendous psychological stress, and I believe that caused the paranoid schizophrenia with which I have been diagnosed and continue to live with today.

I'm incredibly open about my ill health: I'm a disabled veteran. I look by all outward signs normal (except maybe for my astigmatism) but inside I deal with voices which tell me both good and bad things to do – the angel and the devil on my shoulder I wrote about earlier. I have to rely upon common sense when I can't resolve the argument between these two sides of me, and it also helps explain why I talk things out so much in a public manner: I'm trying to rationalize events and situations which are causing great turmoil in my mind.

It's like a dark cloud hanging over me. I am on medication for it, but that doesn't stop the voices. I can't turn them off: they're like a radio, playing constantly in the background in my head. They're like talk radio: they tell me a good and a bad situation, and they're polar opposites, and they'll fight and fight it out until eventually neither side wins but both are worn out from arguing.

I didn't hear these voices until I was about 14. I truly believe that the death of my dad was the trigger which caused me to hear voices. It was building up before then, and was exacerbated since then with all the events which have occurred which I had and will explain here. Going to war didn't help: I agree with the diagnosis of navy doctors that my illness existed prior to me entering the military, but think that it was aggravated by the first Gulf War. My experiences there, and in the navy as a whole, are still to come. But I feel it's important to admit them now – not as an excuse for any of the behavior, but because in reading an autobiography you need to know the man as well as you can to understand the context. I'll freely admit it: I am basically messed up in the head.

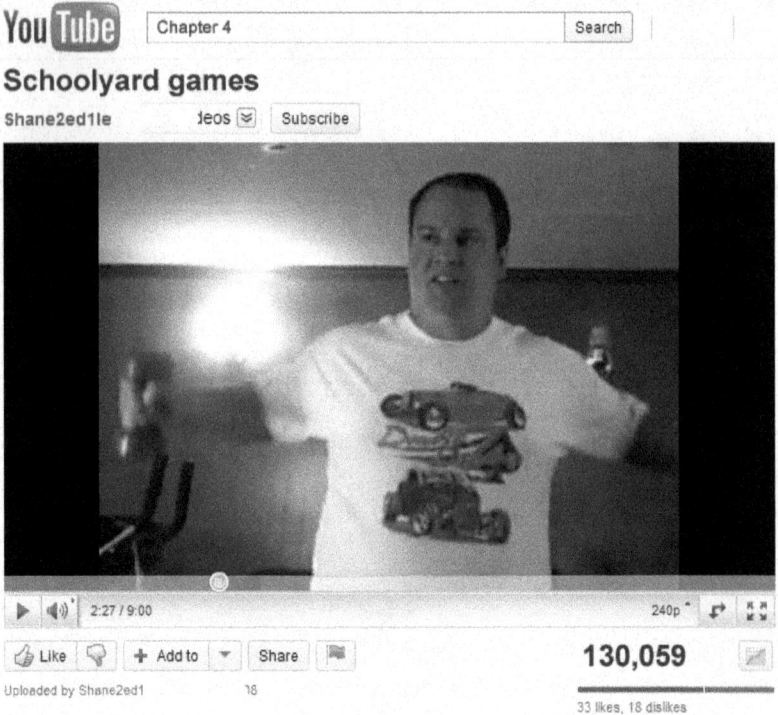

Schoolyard games

Shane2ed1le   Jeos Subscribe

2:27 / 9:00   240p

Like   Add to   Share   **130,059**

Uploaded by Shane2ed1   18

33 likes, 18 dislikes

My medical problems would sometimes mean that I would get into fights at school with other kids. I went to Effingham County and Groves High Schools (the latter was in Garden City, GA), and as I've said, neither of them gave me an easy ride. You don't expect them to when you're a kid going through high school, but my time at school was particularly tough.

When I was in junior high an African-American guy had a problem with me, for some reason. He began calling me names, picking on me, flicking my ears: stupid stuff like that. He told me he wanted to fight me, there and then in the corridor. I didn't encourage him, but I didn't back down either – you don't back down, because it's a sign of weakness – and eventually he started punching me. He got in the first blow, and it rocked my head back. I wasn't expecting him to actually carry through his threat. He tackled me to the floor, and started pounding on me. I wasn't willing to fight back properly because I wasn't looking for any trouble, so I just kept fending him off. A crowd had gathered by then, and obviously when there is a crowd it's conspicuous that something is going on, so the fight was quickly broken up by a teacher. Both of us got taken to the principal's office, and we both ended up getting paddled by him for fighting in the hallway. I still to this day don't know why that guy took a disliking to me; perhaps it was because he thought I looked weird with my astigmatism. Maybe he had some problems of his own and lashed out in the only way he knew how: against someone else. Kids can be very unpredictable, and react in nonsensical ways to situations they aren't yet fully capable of understanding. All I know is that there could have been any number of reasons he decided to fight me that day, and most of them might not have had a single thing to do with me.

The problem was that this was a fairly regular occurrence. Maybe because I was kind of big and hefty, people thought that I would be an interesting guy to fight. Maybe they thought I was fat and couldn't handle myself, and wanted the credibility within the school of taking down a big guy. Maybe they thought I was an outsider because of my religion, or my medical problems, or my mental health problems. Maybe because my parents divorced I was a target. Maybe because my dad died they decided to pick on me. Maybe it was none of these things – but regardless, people kept on asking me to step up and put my fists up. My step-brother Little Roddy would also get challenged, and because we're principled people we would never back down. Sometimes I would get the upper hand and end up victorious, sometimes they would.

These brawls stopped when I took up karate. I guess then I got too good at fighting for people to risk taking me on. I began to learn effective ways to defend myself, and suddenly kids could actually get hurt if they fought me. I remember the day that it changed; when people realized that all the karate I had done meant that you didn't mess with me. It was eighth grade. This guy bumped into me near my locker, and told me to get out of his way. I didn't answer him back, which I guess he took as a personal affront, so he snapped around and pushed me against the wall, his arm up by my neck. He challenged me to a fight there and then, and I said yes. I warned him that I had taken karate, and could really hurt him, but I think he thought I was lying to try and brag my way out of the fight.

I knew that I couldn't embarrass myself. By then I had only just started karate, but I knew the basics. I was ready to prove myself to him, and to everybody else. A crowd gathered round. We grappled for a bit, and the guy managed to get a few punches in on me, but I pushed him away from me and wound up my leg.

I hit him with all my might with a flying roundhouse kick which got him right in the stomach. That put an immediate stop to the fight. He was winded and shocked, and slumped to the floor. I was the winner, but more importantly people knew I was really taking karate and wasn't to be messed with. A PE teacher came up behind me and grabbed me to break up the fight. I didn't realize at the time, though, that it was him, and did a move to get this strange person off me – I thought that it was someone else trying to attack me. I apologized as soon as I knew that it was a teacher, and didn't get in trouble for that.

I did karate for nearly five years. I started in 1982, and ended midway through 1987. In that time I got up to blue belt status, which is just two away from getting a black belt. Like most other things I took an interest in, I also read around the subject. I looked into the samurai, which really interested me, and bought five books on Ninjitsu by Steven K Hayes. All of those were useful in giving me context and honing my technique. The particular style of karate I took was called Chito (or sometimes Shito) Ryu, which is a particularly hard-hitting Japanese style of karate.

There were two kicks which I was good at (and still am, even though I'm less mobile than I was back then): the roundhouse and the hook kick. (I knew all of the kicks: front kicks, side kicks, back kicks, inside and outside crescent kicks, and a spinning heel kick, but I was better with my feet than my hands.) As part of my training, we would go as a karate club to tournaments, and I would do pretty well. Sometimes I would win, sometimes I would lose, but I would always have fun – even if you sometimes got hit a little harder than you would like. Once, one of my friends that I met in the seventh grade called David Pellum was sparring with me. We were being gentle, but still fighting properly and hitting each other. He caught me with a spinning heel kick to the face which really hurt, but I was determined to show him no inkling that he had actually caused me pain, so I laughed at him. Another time we were fooling around with karate equipment and found some Japanese throwing stars, or shuriken. We started tossing them around, and David Pellum kept pretending like he was going to throw one properly at me, but keeping a hold of it. However the third time he faked me out, he lost grip on the shuriken and it flew out of his hand and caught me in the shoulder. It ended up embedding itself in my skin and hitting me in the collarbone. It didn't do any lasting damage, but it hurt an awful lot and I learned to be more careful with dangerous objects like that in the future.

There is still a scar there today, faint though it is, from where the shuriken pierced the skin. I've been an avid photographer – on my first website (more of which later) I uploaded hundreds of photos of myself, showing the different physical scars that you can see on the outside. Of course, I can't show you the internal scars, and those that have left their toll on my psychologically. Those you just have to believe exist.

I enjoyed goofing around in my childhood. I made a home movie when I was younger about a ninja who stole a trophy. I don't remember who recorded it – who was behind the camera – but I know that I was in the starring role as the ninja. I was fighting the good guys to stop them recapturing the trophy I stole. Eventually, these ninjas (who were played by my friends like David and Myron) managed to defeat me and return the trophy to its rightful owners. I sometimes wish I still had that movie to look back on. I think it'd be a good watch today.

You can probably tell I was karate mad. I used to watch a TV show which I think was called The Master, which starred Sho Kosugi, every week. I watched that alongside most TV shows that people watched, like The Dukes of Hazzard, Wonder Woman, Spiderman, Little House on the Prairie and Fame. That last TV show may well be where I got my idea to sing on Youtube from.

Though I liked watching TV, I was one of those outdoors kids.

Me, Myron and David would sometimes hang out in various places during the summer. You could invariably find me anywhere but my own house: it could be at David's house, in the woods, at the Ogeechee River or another swimming hole called Heights Landing. The problem with spending so long outdoors was that my right eye (the one which has astigmatism in it) is very light sensitive. Even today, when I get out into the sunlight from my house or a store, for example, I start blinking a lot. It was the same back then. Of course, blinking can quite easily be misconstrued as winking, which I think got me into a lot of trouble. People would think I was winking when in fact I was innocently blinking. One is done on purpose while the other is done involuntarily. With women I don't mind people misreading that – though I am a one-woman man – but with the men it can be a problem. They take it the wrong way.

The three musketeers as we called ourselves (me, Myron and David) would sometimes hang out with Ray, Donald and Russell Chance. Donald and Ray were real goofy acting, which was actually endearing. They would win you over with their clowning about. Donald would sometimes pick on me; I let him, because he was goofy looking too. I was good though. I never picked on him.

One summer the six of us went all the way up to Forsyth, GA for a change of scene. We were going swimming, as we usually did, and we were at a local river we didn't know. There was this hot looking girl there that we were all staring at, looking like a row of panting dogs with our tongues down to our bellies. I was the only one of the six of us who got up enough courage to go over to this girl and talk to her. I scored! She let me put some sun lotion on her, which was real fun. All the guys were amazed at me, and I was treated as a hero because I had touched a girl.

We'd also go down south to Statesboro, GA to go skating or to the drive-in movies. Sometimes we'd sneak into the movies, because we couldn't afford it. We were very good at never getting caught. Also in Statesboro there was a fair coming to town one summer, and I wanted to go with Lisa. She was my girlfriend at the time, and I liked spending time with her. I managed to hitch a ride from Pineora, GA to Statesboro – which is a long long way – just to see her. Once I was there I was stranded, until her uncle took pity on me and gave me a lift home.

We kept ourselves busy. I used to like going to the school dances either to dance with a girl I liked or just to dance by myself and show off my moves to other girls. Those, rather than the educational parts, were my favorite parts of school life.

I never finished school. I should point that out now. While most people are proud to call themselves high school graduates, all I have to show for it is a GED.

There are various reasons why all I got was a GED and not a high school diploma – least of which was the psychological torment that I went through at school. Losing my dad certainly didn't help either. But there was also the time that I spent recovering from a serious accident which threatened my life more than perhaps any other.

The second miraculous event to happen in my life again almost killed me. Like the Jawbreaker incident, this was an incredibly close pass with death, and I feel tremendously blessed to still be here to be able to talk about it. However unlike the Jawbreaker incident, which happened when I was young and barely conscious of what was going on, this time I was nearly 17 and fully aware of everything, so it sits ingrained on my memory, in full color and horrific detail.

It was August 24, 1986 – just a few weeks before my seventeenth birthday. I was like most kids at that age. I liked to drive around in cars, listening to music, watching the world roll by your window. I liked the wind in my hair, my arm out the window, and I liked to think that I was a movie star. The sort of movie star like James Dean, impressing girls with his ride. Little did I know that I nearly met the same fate James Dean did on that day. I was driving a 1980 Oldsmobile Cutlass Supreme, which is a beautiful slender car with big chrome bumpers front and back. It's essentially a mid-sized car, but it looked great. It almost looked like you could pass it off as a muscle car, which is what I tried to do. I imagined, when I was driving it, that I was driving a Dodge or something similar. Little Roddy was with me in the car.

I had been talking to him about us getting a job together, and we could carpool and drive there, or go on dates together or something. He seemed keen, but he wanted to know that I could handle this car I had. He challenged me to prove it, so I was maybe pushing the limits. I was driving on the roads around Guyton, GA, and had pulled off Highway 17 onto a road that used to be called Old 17 but has since changed its name to Floyd. I was going around 60mph. It was still daylight, and the sun there can be particularly bright. This day it was streaming through the windshield, a white flare of light that turned orange and pink at the edges. The road is banked by trees that fall away from the side of the road down a bit of an incline, so it seems like you're driving halfway up a canopy. The foliage is deep a few feet off the edge of the road, but the sun still finds a way to dart through and cast its light in pinpricks onto the sides of your car. It was a perfect driving day, on a fantastic stretch of road deep in Georgia. The Old 17 is a single-lane road, but each direction has a wide lane to drive in. It's not cramped, but it's not open country either: it's...well, it's just right.

I went around a sharp curve in the road, and I suppose I must've been going a few miles per hour too fast (I've since taken the road at 45-50mph with no problems, as part of my rehabilitation to try and conquer the fear of the tarmac), because I lost control of the car. The back end kicked out, and I couldn't stop the car. I tried – my God, I tried. I'm sure I kept kicking the brakes desperately trying to stop this huge hunk of metal careening off the road and into the undergrowth. They mustn't have worked. I might've been missing the pedals. I don't know. The car went airborne, and I thought this was it. The end. After what seemed like minutes, but must only have been seconds, the car came crashing down into the dirt nose first, and everything jolted. The momentum threw me forward, and my head went cracking into the windshield, popping the whole pane of glass clear out of the car.

The front end of the car crumpled pretty much all the way up to where the windshield would've been. I partly managed to get my arm up to protect myself before my head hit the glass, but it wasn't good enough.

I was later told that I suffered a five inch fracture from my left eyebrow to the top of my head – which left an eighth of an inch gap in my skull. I sustained a concussion. I shaved the entirety of my left eyebrow off and part of the skin on the top of my nose (any lower and it would've been damage taken directly to my eye). I was cut on my right cheek. I had gouges in my hand where the glass had shattered. My right ankle was seriously hurt from debris and the crumpling car. I have a knot behind my right ear, on the back of my head, which is about an inch long, which the doctors still today don't understand. They presume it's misplaced cartilage or bone or something.

By some miracle I managed not to break my neck. Thank God I didn't break my neck, that's all I could think. They initially thought I had: when I first got to the hospital, my neck was supple and tender to palpitation over its entire length. One x-ray of the lateral c-spine showed a questionable area around my C2 and C3 vertebrae, which they thought then and still do think now could have been a small fracture; at the time, they just put on my notes that there was a "possible cervical spine injury". I believe that it's on my neck where the true miracle – beyond me surviving the crash in the first place – happened. When they admitted me to hospital, they noticed this injury, but when they re-examined me the following morning, they couldn't find anything. The problem there disappeared. It was miraculously healed in a night.

I looked a mess after the crash. My head, which had just been forced through a pane of glass at 60mph, was caked in blood which poured from still-fresh wounds. It was lying on the hood of the car. My body was contorted and pinned on the steering wheel, bent double; half-in and half-out of the car. I couldn't move – I was stuck. My neck was twisted at an awkward angle, and anyone passing by would've taken me for decapitated or dead. I was barely conscious. At first I thought I was dead. I thought I was lain out on the hood of my Oldsmobile, completely stone cold dead. I was a goner. I thought that perhaps I was just imagining that I was still lying there – that I was waiting for someone to pick me up and take me to heaven. I was delirious. I was concerned about Little Roddy; I couldn't turn, or open my eyes, or move or shout or scream to check that he was alright. I just had to lie there, waiting for someone to take me to heaven if I was already dead or hospital if I wasn't (and I didn't believe much in the latter at first).

Someone eventually called the ambulance. It must've been someone who was driving along the road and saw the wrecked car. Whether they had a car phone or they had to drive off and find somewhere with a phone, I don't know. But eventually an ambulance arrived with paramedics. I heard the sirens, and as I slowly parted my eyes I saw the flashing lights. Then I knew I wasn't actually dead. I thought "thank God for the physical exercise, the karate, I do", because my physical condition had maybe saved me from the trauma taken when the car came back down to earth.

The paramedics treat the situation they have in front of them. Though I was alive, their first priority was Little Roddy because he didn't have a scratch on him and was more likely to survive. They took me for dead. Looking at me, I don't blame them; I probably looked dead. I was just thankful they came and saved Little Roddy, and was eventually thankful that they helped me.

They took him off to the side and checked him out before they even considered looking at me. They were just within earshot. I could hear them running through the usual medical questions to ascertain that he was okay, then they began talking more gravely. They hushed their voices, and slowed things down. I imagine that they put their hands on Little Roddy's shoulders. They told him I was probably dead.

At that point my survival instinct kicked in.

I found my voice once more, and though I still couldn't move, I shouted out "no! The hell I am not! Get me the hell out of here!"

I think I passed out from the pain and the exertion of telling them I was still alive. Maybe I was still conscious, but everything is such a blur that I have to rely on the accident reports and other people's testimony for what happened next.

At some point my mom turned up. When she arrived, it turns out that I was out of the car and fighting with the paramedic. She asked, she says, why I was struggling with him and the paramedic told her that I was being abusive and cussing. I can't believe that's true. What I think must've happened is that I was saying that I was in pain, and that "it hurts, dammit!" After all, I ended up with scars all over my body as a result: it's not like it was a cakewalk, getting away from a totaled car. The paramedics asked me if I had been drinking – they presumed, as I suppose anyone would when they are called out to a car accident with a young kid at the side of the road, that I had probably had a couple of beers. In my delirium, not properly understanding the undertone of their question, I said that I had. My mom asked me what I had been drinking. I told her truthfully: water. I was less than keen that the ambulance workers were going to put a neck brace on me, even though they reassured me that it was for my own safety and to prevent any further neck damage. I kept slipping in and out of consciousness. I remember my mom telling the paramedics to just take me to the hospital and do whatever they needed to do and stop asking me questions. I don't remember the journey there.

The next thing I know I've woken up in the hospital later that day and my mom is by my bedside. The records tell me that I was admitted at 10:31pm to Memorial Medical Center in Savannah, GA. She told me I was in an accident, and needed to rest, and everything would be alright. She was right. Though the doctors lied about my condition, and didn't acknowledge the five inch fracture in my skull, for example, on the medical records, I slowly but surely got better. It was a miracle from God.

"Why didn't I break my neck?" is a question I keep asking myself to this day. Only God knows. God healed me, and to this day I don't suffer from any neck pain, and can still lift weights up to 55 pounds, a dumbbell on each arm. With the Lord's help I've tried to recover. I used to play a load of sports from the age of about 10: basketball, soccer and baseball. I couldn't play that well (because of my eye problems), and sometimes I'd get injured. The coach would always tell me to shake it off and carry on, and that's what I did after the accident too. I hit the windshield so hard that I have memory problems, but I had that sort of problem before the accident too, so it's only made it worse, not caused it.

I was only in hospital for a little over a day. I spent two nights – the first night I was admitted, it was late. The second night they kept me in to make sure I was alright, and so I was discharged on August 26. I walked out of Memorial (though I think they tried to make me use a wheelchair) with stitches in my right hand and ankle and swollen pride that I had survived.

I was never right since then, though. That accident affected me, and added to the catalogue of my woes.

You Tube | Chapter 5 | Search

Getting on with my life

selee1shane   Subscribe

1:29 / 4:18   240p

Like   + Add to   Share

130,059

Uploaded by selee1shar

It would be unfair to say that once I left school I was only flipping burgers. I tried a variety of jobs. I worked for the airport Days Inn in Garden City, GA before I joined the navy. That was a *hard* job. I had to get up about 5am every morning and ride my bike the long miles into work. It got tiresome real quick. The guy the hotel set to train me didn't care about doing it right and making sure I knew what I was doing, so I became unmotivated. That, coupled with me being unsure as to how to actually do the things they wanted me for, meant that I got fired.

I worked in a bunch of fast food restaurants for a while after high school finished. The work wasn't the best, but it was still okay. You got to meet a lot of people in a day, and you occasionally got free food, and you got to make people happy. It didn't have the best job satisfaction in the world, but it certainly wasn't the worst that you could possibly have. Ultimately, though, when you're a kid who had to resit the sixth and 11th grades in school and only just managed to get his GED, you have to make a difficult decision. If you're from small town Georgia, it's unlikely that you're going to get beyond a certain position in life, with my circumstances. Sooner, rather than later, I had to come to the realization that my life wasn't necessarily going to be like the movies. I wasn't going to be able to segue from small town to big city. I would have to abandon my old school friends and the life I had with them, driving around the countryside, playing on hay bales and so on, or I would be stuck there.

There are glass ceilings in this world. Occasionally, people get enough vertical velocity to be able to break through those ceilings and achieve something more. Occasionally they manage to do something which people thought was beyond them, and people are happy for it. Anyone *can* do that: I genuinely believe that. If you start off with a normal life, and you continue to have a normal life during your childhood, you have the ability and the possibility to break through that ceiling. I didn't have those things. I was a kid who lost his father when he was young, whose parents divorced. I had mental and physical trouble. I was picked on at school. In reality, with my grades and with my circumstances, I was never going to get beyond the state boundary. So I had to think long and hard, and I realized that though I wasn't going to be able to break out of the rut by working up from within Georgia (the best I could probably have done at the time was become the manager at the local McDonalds), I could travel and see foreign countries – even just see beyond the border with Florida – by joining the navy.

I was 19, and I had heard from a few friends that the recruiter was going to be in town in the next few weeks. I carefully considered everything that I had: my mom, my step-brothers, a few friends from school who I used to meet up with every so often, my job packing sausages at the Roger Wood Packing Company in Savannah, GA. I considered what the navy could give me: a ticket away from Georgia, a new group of friends, an ability to succeed. The choice was clear. Shane Edward Lee was going to join the navy.

I started the process. The couple of weeks wait passed by and I became resolved to do it. I was going to sign up. The recruiter from the navy came along to my neighborhood and set up a fold-out table and some papers with a roll banner on the forecourt of the local gas station. It was a bright sunny day bleaching down on his uniform. He looked heaven sent.

In the two weeks leading up to the recruiter coming to town I had talked over the decision with a few of my friends. My best friend David Pellum decided he was going to join me: two kids on the seven seas!

Our dream of sailing the oceans together rapidly fell apart. As we queued in line, swatting away the flies buzzing around our faces, it became obvious that the recruitment process was actually that – a process, not a rubberstamping of anyone who bothered to wait in line and smile politely at the buzz-cut recruiting officer.

David went first, and was rapidly picked apart by this navy man. He was asked questions about his high school education, his fitness and his personal life. It didn't look good. He wasn't educated enough; he wasn't fit enough; the recruiter didn't think he had the personality to make it – and to survive – in the navy. The recruiter told him that he would take on his application, if David really wanted him to, but that it was unlikely to go anywhere. It would be a waste of his time and of David's too. David was disheartened, as you would expect. He'd been led to believe that the navy was his big ticket out of Savannah and around the world, and in about three minutes flat it had been crushed. He didn't know what to do, so he turned around and he walked home, dejected. I began to foresee that I would be doing the same, too. David hadn't had the health problems which had blighted my younger days; he was, to my eyes, a better fit in the navy. He was the person I looked up to, as I suppose everyone looks up to their friend (he may in reality have not been all that much better than me, but people like myself are much more likely to see themselves as inferior to others rather than superior, even if it's not necessarily the case).

I gulped after I saw David being sent home with his tail between his legs. I was next in line.

The guy wasn't hugely fearsome or anything, but he wasn't overly welcoming either. He put an arm straight out and beckoned me over, gruffly shouting "next!" as he did so. I had a pile of my papers with me (school records, job references, things like that), and I subconsciously used them as a shield, holding them up close against me. I was the meek young boy once again, confronted by this grown man in a crisply starched navy uniform.

Luckily he wasn't quite as abrupt with me as he was with David. He looked over my papers, and talked to me a bit about my childhood and why I wanted to join the navy. The flop sweat which I initially had – partly caused by the bleaching sun, partly by the fear he had struck into my heart – abated and dried in the heat. The recruiter was more positive: though I had my GED, rather than a high school diploma, that would be enough, he thought. In fact, he said, the whole GED system was designed just after World War II to help veterans get back into civilian life and get decent jobs. While they'd been away, they'd lost out on a decent education, and most jobs post-war were beginning to have a minimum skill set. The GED was designed to prove that even those veterans who had not completed their schooling could take an active place in society. Perversely, having a GED rather than a normal high school diploma might have helped me get a place on boot camp. I went home happy that day, with the recruiter saying that so long as there weren't any hitches, I should be able to report for boot camp later that year.

There weren't any problems, and I got a letter through the mail telling me where and when to report to boot camp. I was ecstatic: here was a chance to really better myself, and to escape. David was happy for me, but sad that I'd be leaving him and Savannah.

I began to have strange religious dreams about boot camp. I believed that my drill sergeant was the Lord, and that the enemy we were being trained to fight was the Devil. I was being guided safely through all the drills, and was being kept healthy by Jesus. I dreamt that I got through boot camp with flying colors.

I was excited, and packed up my stuff to go to boot camp. It all fit in one bag, and when I turned up there boot camp was everything I imagined and more. It was in Chicago, and we got to fly there and back – which was enough of a new experience to be exciting. I was able to escape from my home town for the first time apart from vacations, and I began to feel like I was a man of the world. The dream was coming true. There were no problems; there was no hassle. I felt like I belonged.

While I was waiting to meet up with everyone at boot camp I was accosted by some Jehovah's Witnesses. I dislike them: they proselytize way too much for my liking, and their view of religion is very blinkered and completely at odds with what I've been taught and what I know as one of God's two witnesses is right.

These Jehovah's Witnesses didn't believe in serving in the military, even though it's one of the most patriotic things you can do, and told me I was wrong for wanting to join the navy. We got into a discussion, and they left before I could properly put my mind across. They were so closeted.

When I got home that night what they had said stuck in the back of my mind and drilled into my brain. I couldn't get to sleep for thinking about it. So I got on my knees and prayed. I asked God if they were right and I was misled, or whether I was right and they were wrong.

I had what I can only describe as an incredibly lucid dream that night.

I dreamt of going to boot camp. It was the day we were being issued with our clothes. I was standing in an enormous line waiting for the uniform like everyone else. Eventually – after what seemed like forever – I got to the front of the line. I was given my pile of clothes, and in the dream I felt uncomfortable. I had all these words pent up inside of me, and needed to let them loose. I told the man who gave me my uniform all about the Jehovah's Witnesses and what they had said, and he didn't do anything in reply. He just waved me through. I ended up joining the navy in the dream. I told them about an eye surgery I had when I was 12, but decided against admitting that I suffered from astigmatism. Of course, they caught it at the MEPS station right away. They still waved me through though – to my astonishment – and I took the oath and everything. I was in the navy!

I finished up the community service I had been given for burglarizing a house (more on that in a later chapter), and learned my lesson, and wrote a long and deliberative essay about why I wanted to join the navy. I explained in the essay that I had been taught what was right and what was wrong, and that I wouldn't burglarize anyone ever again and just wanted a career and wanted to do *something* with my life.

Most incredibly, this happened almost exactly as it did in the dream when I got to boot camp proper. It was like I had had a déjà vu dream. God wanted me in the military, and would help me to make it through. I knew that then.

Boot camp was fun. I did alright in it. Truth be told, I didn't try overly hard; I went through it with relative ease. I was made the religious petty officer, which was a job close to my heart. The job of the religious petty officer is basically to be a rabble rouser: I was in charge of getting people into church every Sunday. I did that fairly well. I helped people get in touch with their spiritual side, which was a job I took very seriously because religion had such an important effect on my own life.

We went to a Jewish service off-base, once. That wasn't normal during boot camp – in fact, it was unheard of. We got to leave the base for that. There was a problem one time we went to the Jewish service, though. It turns out that the rabbi conducting the Jewish service had been persecuted by Christians when he was growing up. I didn't know this, and I was just trying to learn more about a different religion so that I could better respect their beliefs. We were allowed to ask questions. I innocently (I thought) asked a question about the Holy Trinity. The rabbi got upset. He attacked me. I want to make it clear that I was only trying to understand the Jewish perspective on what was an important aspect of my religion, not to start an argument. It all worked out in the end, luckily, but it was embarrassing and awkward at the time that such an innocent question blew up in my face so quickly.

There was a woman who worked with the rabbi. I had a weird dream about her. Sexual. I also dreamt about a large heavy-set man with silver hair who tried to force himself on me. I think that could've been about the pastor who put his hand in my buttocks.

I got to A-school next, which tries to skill you up in preparation for when you join the navy proper. I was being trained up to be an electrician. I passed – just barely – but was told that you get your hands-on training out while in the fleet.

I was steadily becoming paranoid about the first Gulf War. I already had sleeping problems during school; I was tested by the navy for narcolepsy, which turned up inconclusive. I was ready to leave because of a lack of sleep and misgivings about going to war, but the night before the narcolepsy test I got a good night's sleep. I guess that was a sign from God that I should continue.

The test was strange. It was administered by a psychologist on the base. The study made me sleep, but I couldn't. For some reason they gave me a clean bill of health, though she assured me that I could follow up at my next command if the problem continued or got worse. I was forging ahead in the navy, come hell or high water.

I got to my command, the USS Saipan, and everything started off fairly smoothly. But things quickly went downhill. I started getting harassed by a guy called Ben Campbell, who kept teasing me that I was gay. When you're onboard a ship, that sort of thing can really blight your future and make it difficult. He made it awkward for me to get on with the other guys, and it got to the stage where we eventually got into a fight over it. He slammed me against a tin wall, and I hit him upside the head, which I thought would get me respect. It didn't.

There were other problems too. One guy got electrocuted almost as soon as we arrived. That concerned me. Didn't they know what they were doing?, I thought to myself? I was worried about working with people who were so clumsy, but I still showed up every morning for them to train me. They didn't. There must have been some miscommunication, because I would report every morning for them to train me (or tell me what to do, even), but they always made me go out on the job alone, like they believed I knew everything there was to know about the job. I was just starting out! I didn't know anything! I didn't know the job, or the ship. Even if I had understood what the job entailed, I still didn't know my way around this ship. I should surely have been trained a little, I thought, but I still ploughed on.

I went to mess duty, and did whatever they told me to do. I went from washing the dishes to serving high-ranking officers their meals. I cleaned the state rooms and maintained the logic circuits for the elevators. I did each job I was given to the best of my ability; I did it the best I could with limited training. All this while I was still concerned – a problem exacerbated by them not really knowing they needed to train me – that they didn't know what they were doing. I thought they were trying to kill me, or electrocute me. They weren't willing to train with me; they weren't willing to work with me. I hadn't done anything wrong! They blamed me for them not training me, which is a patently ridiculous thing for them to say. They didn't seem to appreciate that I had mental problems. In A-school, you are only shown everything quickly and once. You're expected to pick it up immediately. That might be fine for normal people, but I'm not normal. I was in a car accident with a five inch fracture in my skull. That was bound to affect me a little. I fought hard against it, and tried to overcome my handicap and keep going.

I wasn't someone who had photographic memory. I did, however, develop supernatural hearing, I could hear people talking about me. Some was good, but most was bad. That hurt. I knew they didn't want to work with me. I knew they thought that I was being lazy and that I didn't know what to do, but they didn't seem to appreciate that I wasn't being told what was needed of me.

They made it very awkward for me. Every morning when I came into the divisional work area on the ship, all my shipmates would suddenly stop talking and stare at me. It was as if they had turned into a pack of animals, and realized I was the one with a weakness. They rounded on me.

I carried on, though I wasn't happy.

I didn't try to evangelize my shipmates. I didn't thrust it upon them that I was one of the two witnesses (though they knew from my role as petty officer and the fact that I went to First Christian Church in Norfolk, VA every Sunday that I was religious). The only people I told about my belief were the general pastor at the base and the local pastor. I told the psychiatrist in the navy about it all, but I left out some details at the time because I thought it might be harmful to my proving that I was one of the two witnesses. I think that's why I was diagnosed with paranoid schizophrenia: because I was so totally focused on the single objective of proving that I was a witness. I was wholly focused on that, but now I'm assured that I am one of the two witnesses I can multitask once more. I reckon that one day – far off – I might be called to Jerusalem by God. I told my Sunday school teacher about the dream I had of seeing the throne of God in heaven, too, but I was clear about telling others. I never persecuted unbelievers. I wouldn't do that. However, I am a firm believer that any person who believes in a religion can express their belief in that religion so long as they don't break the laws of the state concerning moral issues.

Freedom of expression means I can tell you what I believe up to three times. That much is clear. You too can refuse to believe me or agree with me, but you have to tolerate my expression of my religion just the same way that I have to tolerate your belief even if I don't agree.

As long as we're in agreement on what is moral and what isn't, what's right and what's wrong, and as long as we can live together in peace we're fine.

For example, I studied Kabala a little bit, but had a fundamental problem with it. I tried it, then stopped doing it. And this is the thing: if you stop, you invariably run into a patch of bad luck. For example, when I stopped Kabala, my car got wrecked.

I was taught by the navy to deal with on-board firefighting. I even went to A-school for it. But like most things, I was never allowed to show or train my shipmates how to do it. I wasn't used to my full potential. In fire drills, instead of being on the front line fighting the fire, they'd make me a messenger, ferrying pointless alerts and alarms to different people.

I would show up to work every day and ask what we were going to do that day. I was willing to work: I wanted to, badly. But I was never trained, and I was never used properly.

My shipmates even *got caught* avoiding training me, but they somehow managed to weasel themselves out of trouble by banding against me and placing the blame squarely at my feet. I didn't know what to do – but it wasn't my fault. Electricity isn't something you can just play at: it's dangerous, and you need to know what to do with it properly. On the odd occasions they did tell me what to do, I listened intently and followed orders. If I didn't understand what they were saying, I asked for clarification to better do my job.

Despite all this I wasn't appreciated. I was never appreciated. I was made the black sheep, and got put on all the crappy jobs. I was made to clean the bathroom duty (to be put on head as they called it, from the days in the old navy when the bathroom was always at the head of the ship), or made to paint the ship. I was given all the menial jobs, but I did what I was told without outward complaint. They even moved me over to another division, so toxic was the atmosphere. It started out rough there, too. I had to paint the boiler, which was hard taxing work. They realized at this division that I was a hard worker and only needed guidance and teaching; they realized that I would pitch in without complaint and that all I needed was more hands-on training (especially beyond that which I got at A-school).

The problem with A-school is that they show you everything you need to know really fast. The whole learning process is condensed down into a matter of a few months. It's no real way to learn anything – at least not concretely, where it'll stick in your brain. It's only in repetition of tasks that you truly learn what to do. Either my shipmates knew what they were doing but acted like they didn't, or they were altogether more worrying and didn't know themselves what they were doing.

Either way, I never got trained beyond A-school, which is a sad state of affairs. It was problematic, because I was never that great at school anyway. I was an average student. I was handicapped by the car accident I had. That made it even harder. They weren't exactly accommodating to the problems I had.

I'm not against the military as a whole. I know that not every person goes through things the same way, and I know that in many ways I was an exceptional circumstance. But there *has* to be a way for men who are working together to get along and not harass each other. There has to be. If not, then there needs to be a system in place which makes them get along. You can't be prejudiced, especially when you're in such close quarters with people like you are in the navy.

I'm sure it was my bad eye which made all my shipmates uneasy. I can't do anything about that. It's a physical blight. I can't turn it on and off. They didn't understand why I was in a good mood no matter what they threw at me. They didn't understand why I was such a positive person; they didn't know what I hoped to achieve from it. I was trying to be positive even though I was being done wrong; I owed it to my faith in Jesus to do that. I didn't force them to believe as I believed. Don't get me wrong: I didn't hide my belief under a bushel either – I wasn't ashamed of it. But we don't have to persecute, nor do we have to be persecuted if we are willing to try and get along with each other and live good lives.

It wasn't all bad, the navy experience.

I met a girl – Sheena. While I was dating Lisa before I joined the navy, I had a dream. I was getting bored of Lisa – she was being difficult and standoffish and cold towards me, and I sort of knew it was coming to the end. So I prayed to God and asked him to bring me an Asian girl. Japanese, Chinese, Vietnamese, Korean or even Arabic – I didn't mind. I wasn't racist or anything like that. I just wanted a pretty Asian girlfriend with long black hair. In the dream I got a girlfriend, and about a year later when I was in the navy I was entranced by a girl who looked exactly like the girl I had dreamt about. It was Sheena.

Our eyes met across the bow of her ship. She was stationed on another ship, but by a strange turn of luck her ship and mine ended up going to two ports together in Israel while on tour. I wanted to get married in Jerusalem – I told her so – but she didn't seem so keen. I was worried I had gotten her pregnant: on leave in Spain we had a three-day holiday in a place called Palma where she truly melted my heart. But we had sex under a tree without protection and I was worried that we might've conceived. It turns out that we didn't.

Going to Israel itself was a big bonus for me. I truly enjoyed the two visits there that we made as a ship. The first time we went, we went via Hragada, Egypt, and anchored off Haifa. I managed to wangle shore leave, and did a whistle-stop two day tour of the Holy Land. Then and there I made a pact with myself that I would come back some day, and it happened sooner than I could ever have imagined. The second time we went there it was for two weeks, which was plenty of time for me to properly explore the country which was outlined in the Bible. It was great, but I was concerned because the USS Saipan went port side into the dock and didn't anchor like usual. I was worried that this made us a target for Saddam Hussein, and that gave me palpitations.

Things began to get all a little bit too much for me. Woe after woe started to pile up on my shoulders, and made me nervous. My granddads (both of them) died around this time too – 1991 – which only added to my stress. I was trying to grieve, while enduring the lashings and bullying of my shipmates, and suffering from psychotic episodes related to all the stress. I began getting tetchy and dissociated with the rest of those people around me. I was worried I was falling apart. Something had to break.

My life may appear sometimes to be like a soap. I'd rather it wasn't that way (even though it makes for a good autobiography). I would like to live a quiet life with God. Through all the problems I tried to maintain my strong relationship with Him and make the right choices. I tried to treat people right. "And if a man also strive for masteries, *yet* is he not crowned, except he strive lawfully" says 2 Timothy 2:5, and that's what I try to do. If I made a mistake in my life, I admit it, and try my best not to make the same mistake again. If it's something that can or could hurt someone, then I try all I can to not do it in the first place. People are bound to get hurt when you make mistakes in love, but I never hurt anyone on purpose. I live for loving people as brothers and sisters, as the Bible tells me. I know that we're all one blood and flesh, through the body of our dear Lord and savior Jesus Christ.

The problem is that those people that I shared my navy experience with, by and large, weren't the same. They didn't share my positive outlook on life. They made my life hell, and something had to break. Eventually, it did. Life changing experience number three, little did I know then, was just around the corner.

It was pay day, September 15th, 1994, and I had just gotten £280.00 out of the ATM on the base. I was planning on going out for the night. I met a serve girls I might not – all I wanted to do was have a good time, and $250 in my pocket was going to ensure that I would have a good time.

My plan was simple; I was going out, so I wanted to put clean clothes on for the night. I would go back to my short stab, shower and put on some nice clothes, and head out my wallet (hoping that the banknotes I had in my pocket). The barracks were fairly quiet – people were going about their own business, or preparing to head out or go out on the town.

I got back to the barracks and had it seen that many people on the journey back. It was a short walk. I got into my room, I took

It was payday, September 15th, 1994, and I had just gotten $250.00 out of the ATM on the base. I was planning on going out for the night. I might meet some girls, I might not – all I wanted to do was have a good time, and $250 in my pocket was going to ensure that I would have a good time.

My plan was simple. I was going out, so I wanted to get cleaned up for the night. I would go back to my room, grab a shower and put on some nice clothes, and head out, my wallet bulging from the banknotes I had in my pocket. The barracks were fairly quiet – people were going about their own business, or preparing themselves to go out on the town.

I got back to the barracks and hadn't seen that many people on the journey back. It was a short walk. I got into my room. I took off my shirt, and went to the bathroom area with my travel bag. I put the key to my room in the travel bag and began to get washed up at the sink. I lathered up my hands and washed my face and under my arms. I washed all the usual places. I managed to get a bit of soap in my eye, which stung a lot, but I wiped it out then bathed it in some cool water I pooled between my hands. I put my soap back in my travel bag, then left it on the side of the sink as I went for a leak. I can't have been more than 20 seconds.

I got back and grabbed my wash bag and walked back to my room. I dug my hand into the bag to find the key. It was missing. I went back to the bathroom and had a quick search around the floor and in the sink. I had a thorough look through the travel bag. The key wasn't there; it definitely wasn't there.

No problem, I supposed. It must've fallen out and someone picked it up. It'll turn up.

I went down to the main floor (my room was on the third floor of the barracks; each floor in the building was about 11-12 feet high. Your average house has floors seven and a half feet tall from floor to ceiling) to ask the guy on watch if there was a master key.

He said that there wasn't a master key. All the rooms had their own separate locks.

Okay, I reasoned. "Could you lend me a shirt for the night until I can figure out how to get back into my room?"

"Sorry boss," he said. There weren't any spare uniforms available.

Did he know somewhere I could sleep for the night?, I asked him.

He didn't know that either.

Now I began to worry. I was stuck outside my room with absolutely nowhere to sleep for the night, no shirt on my back and no money for a motel room. I had taken the $250 out of my pocket and put it – as well as my ATM card – on the desk in my room. I wouldn't need it, would I? I was just getting washed. Stupid, stupid Shane.

I began thinking laterally. Maybe the old people who were originally in the barracks might have a master key. I went looking for them, or for anyone else other than the guy on watch, to see if they could help me. No luck.

I thought rationally. Base security might be able to do something.

I trudged across the base to their security hut and asked if they could do anything. I was pretty much blanked and left to get on with it. They simply weren't interested.

I went back to the barracks. I had found a pair of thick screwdrivers: industrial things, really. I would try and lever the door open, breaking and entering my own room in the barracks.

No matter how hard I pushed the screwdrivers in, I couldn't bust the door. It was staying well and truly shut. I slammed my fist onto the door and became exasperated. I had nowhere to go. I was stuck, separated from a night out – from a bed and my own property, even – by a paltry door.

I was at my wit's end. Suddenly, like a spark, I remembered that I had opened the window because it was a close night and the barracks would get really warm. I wasn't sure that I had fully shut it when I left the room: I thought I might've just let it lean to. I figured if I could get onto the roof, I could simply lower myself down to the ledge and check the window. If it was open, I could try and get in. If not, then at least I knew. I could easily climb back onto the roof and get down the same way that I got onto it in the first place.

I had to know which one was my room, of course. It wouldn't look right if I turned up hanging from a ledge outside one of my navy colleagues' windows, trying to force their window open. So I counted the number of rooms from my room to the end of the hall, tapping my fingers on each door as I passed to make sure I counted right. I got to the end of the hall, which was at the back of the barracks building. I made my way outside and counted the same number along to what I was certain was my window. I looked up at the building and saw that I could safely lower myself down to my window, and stand (if I was careful) with my toes on the window ledge. I went around the other side of the building and climbed the outdoor steps, which only went to the third floor of the building. I needed to get to the roof. This was where things got hairy.

There was an opening on the third floor which itself had a solid ledge. There was no access to the roof – at least, there was no easy access. I was going to have to climb into this opening, onto the ledge and climb on it to get to the roof. That was the only choice.

That bit was easy enough. I managed to get onto the ledge and scramble up with little difficulty, and once more counted the rooms along. I really didn't want to get this bit wrong. I thought that after all the trouble I had with people in the navy, the last thing I needed was to be caught appearing to peek into someone else's room. It would've been the end of me and my reputation. I got down on my belly, and slowly rolled myself towards the edge of the building. I rotated myself so that my legs were dangling over the edge, and began to slowly use my upper body strength to lower myself off the building.

I was getting close to my window ledge. My face, which had at first been above the roof of the building, was now in line with the top of my window. My arms felt fine: they could handle my body weight hanging from them. I lowered myself a little more. I could see my ATM card through the window, and my clothes which I had laid out on my bed to go out in. I would be able to go out in Norfolk after all.

I lowered myself another few inches. I was now maybe only four or six inches away from the ledge. This was going well. Four or six inches is less than a single step up a staircase. It's *nothing*. A staircase is about eight inches: this was half a step. It was simple. I was sure to be back in my room, safe.

All I had to do was drop down the few inches and land on the ledge. Simple. Done.

My fingers stretched as long as they could, shortening the drop even more. I let go of the roof to get onto the ledge.

That's all I remember.

I flickered my eyes when I woke up in the emergency room. It hurt to breathe. It hurt to *see*.

I've figured out since that I fell something like 24½ feet.

I can reach the roof of my house when I'm fully stretched out – if I really strain far, that is. That's seven and a half feet. Using that, I can extrapolate that on the barracks building the distance from the roof to the ledge was eight feet. The window ledge itself was three feet – maybe at most three and a half, but nothing more. That itself is 11 feet. The roof at the barracks, though, had a ledge running around it that was at least a foot thick.

I reckon, all in, that barracks building was over 32 feet tall. That's a big fall.

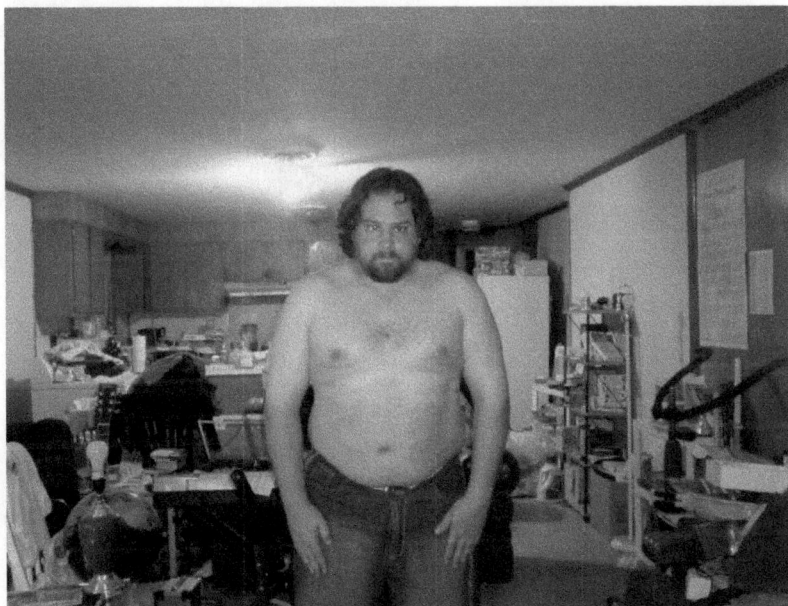

A GOOD BOOK

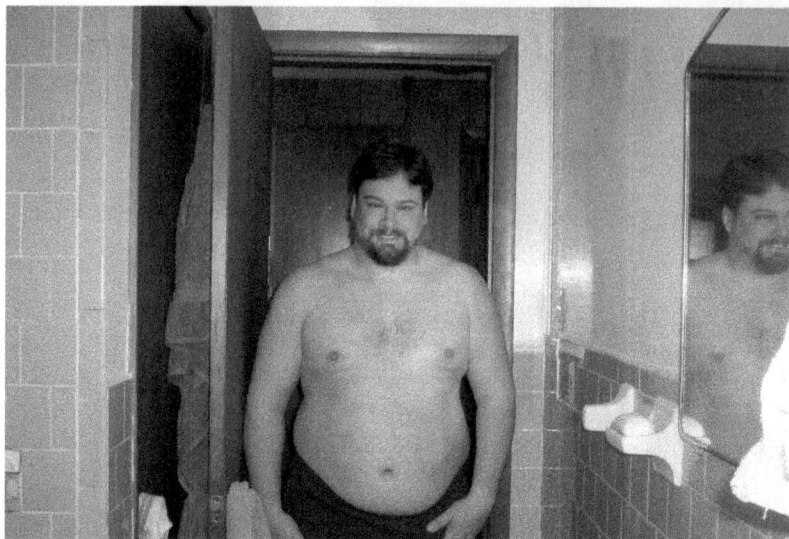

A GOOD BOOK

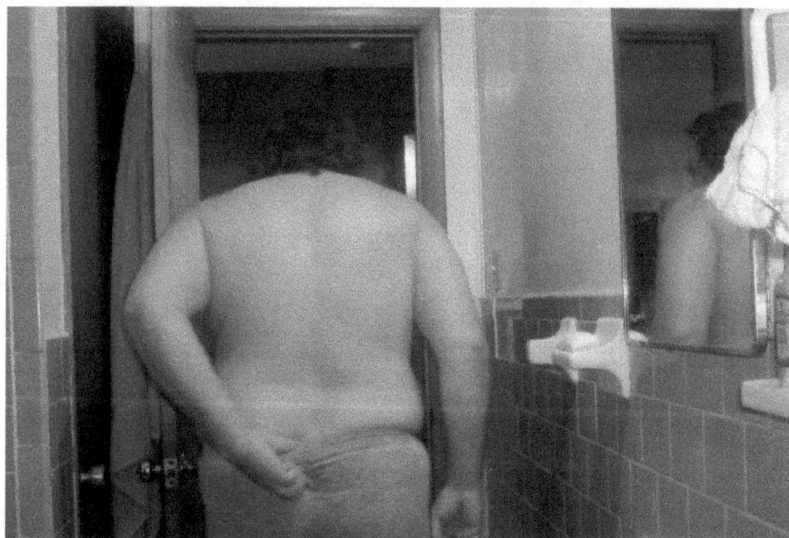

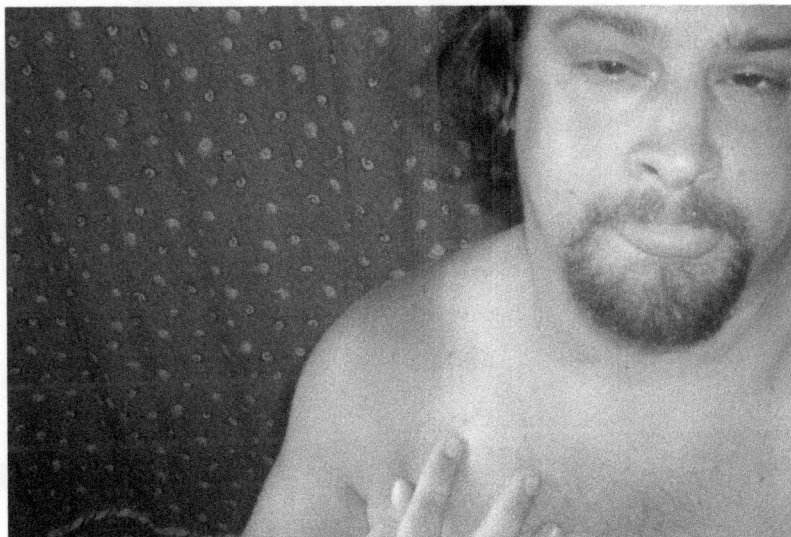

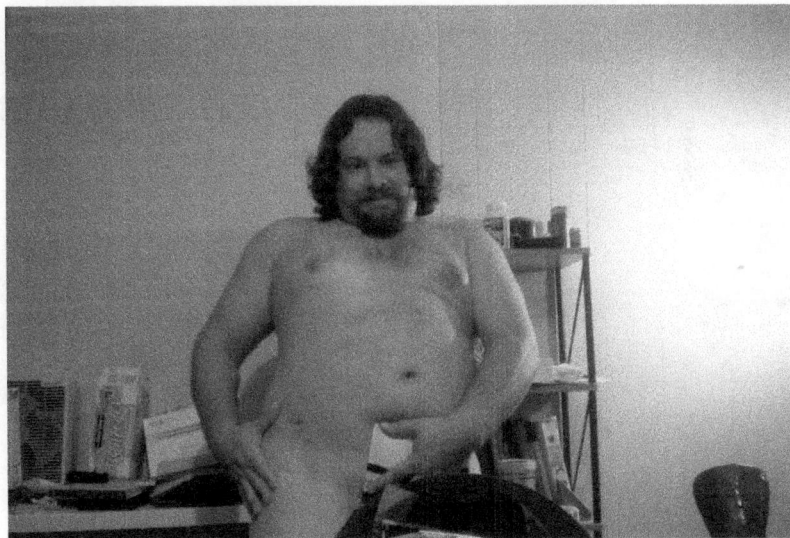

A GOOD BOOK

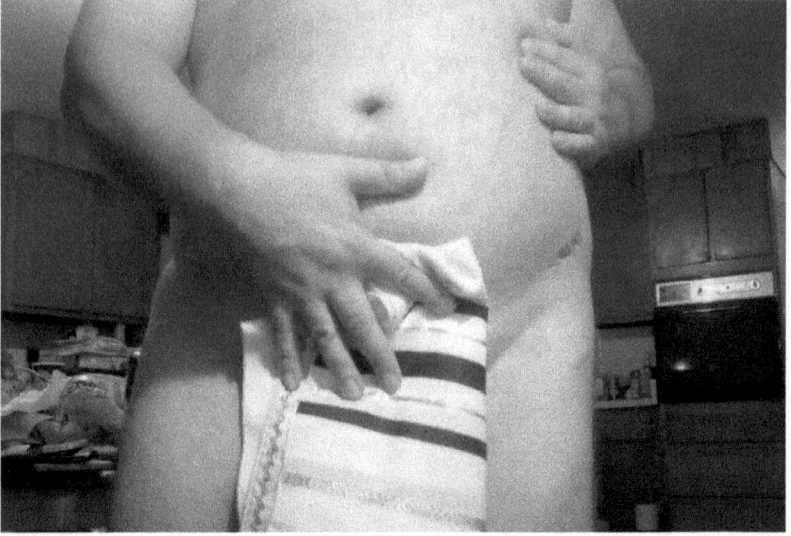

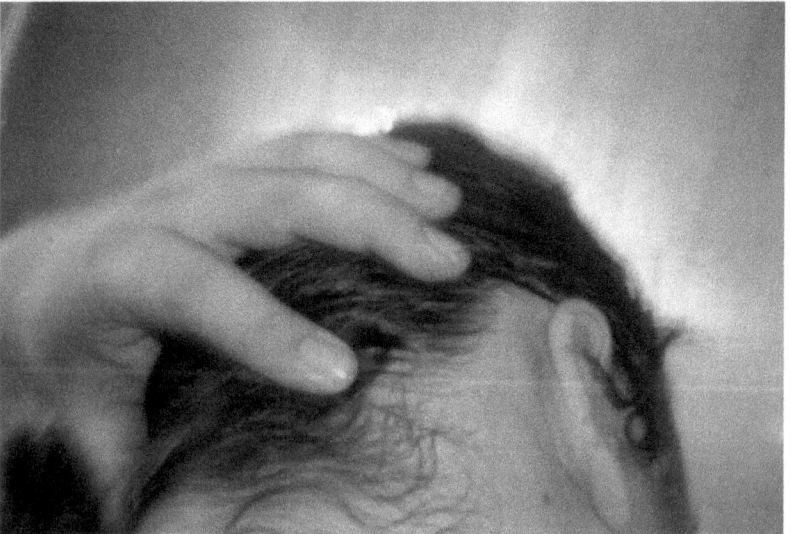

89

SHANE EDWARD LEE

SAVANNAH, GEORGIA

ハ・ウ・
LEE, SHANE
238841-3
W. BROWN, M. D.
E. F. DOWNING, M. D.

HISTORY AND PHYSICAL

ADMITTED: 8-24-86

CHIEF COMPLAINT: "MOTOR VEHICLE ACCIDENT WITH HEAD TRAUMA"

PRESENT ILLNESS: This is a 16-year-old white male who was apparently the driver of
                         an automobile involved in an accident in which the windsheild was
apparently broken out on the driver and passenger side. Patient apparently had some loss
of consciousness, nausea, and vomiting at the scene. He now complains of headache, neck
pain, right wrist pain and has had nausea and vomiting in the ER.

PAST HISTORY: Family denies medical trouble including, heart, lungs, diabetes,
                         epilepsy, or asthma. They state he is not followed by a doctor
regularly for anything, has had no surgery, and is on no medications. There are no known
drug allergies.

FAMILY HISTORY: Noncontributory

PERSONAL/SOCIAL: Patient states he does not drink or smoke cigarettes, he states
                         he has not been drinking tonight.

REVIEW OF SYSTEMS: Unremarkable

PHYSICAL EXAM:

VITAL SIGNS: B/P 160/80, pulse 84, respirations 18.

GENERAL: Somewhat lethargic but arousable white male in mild distress,
                         complaining of headache and neck pain.

HEENT: PERRL, EOMI, conjunctivae and sclerae normal. No hemotympanum
                         on either side. Pharynx normal, no apparent loose teeth, no blood
in the mouth. There is blood in the left ear but there is an avulsion-type laceration on
the superior aspect of the left ear helix. There is no blood in the canal. He has
multiple abrasions and lacerations, all superficial. One contused area over the left
brow. He has an avulsed area of tissue in the left eyebrow which is superfial. There are
superficial minor lacerations over the nose and both cheeks.

NECK: Supple, tender to palpation posteriorly over its entire length,
                         moreso over the C2-3 region.

CHEST: Clear to A, rib palpation reveals no tenderness, no outward sign
                         of trauma.

...CONTINUED...

90

Pt returns p 30 days conleave, currently awaiting med Board 3 months s/p injury. Desires to go to cane ambulation rather than crutch assistance

PE: pin sites from pelvic ex-fix well healed.

(L) Ankle: minimal edema.
mild tenderness c̄ inversion stress

ROM	DF	PF	INV	EV
(L)	15°	25°	5°	5°

X-rays: well healing fx, no displacement

N/V intact.

A/P Pt well healing 3 months s/p from fall (4 stories high) sustained Pelvic Fx and (L) ankle trimalleolar injury. Doing well minimal tenderness/discomfort c̄ ambulation. Pt will remain in MED HOLD Pending PEB Board determination. f/u in 6-8 wks.

Limit-X
SH80
Shtock

MEMORIAL M●ICAL CENTER
SAVANNAH, GEORGIA

PAGE TWO
CONTINUATION ON
LEE, SHANE
238841-3
W. BROWN, M. D.
E. F. DOWNING, M. D.

HISTORY AND PHYSIC.

ABDOMEN: Soft, positive bowel sounds, :   nausea and vomiting during, no
                  real tenderness, guarding, or   ⌐nd. No outward side of trauma.

GU: Normal circumcised male, teste   escended bilaterally, no blood in
                  the meatus.

RECTAL: Normal, heme-negative.

EXTREMITIES: Multiple lacerations and tende: over dorsum of right hand. He
                  has a hematoma and abrasion ov.   ⌐e left hip. There is an
avulsion of soft tissue on the medial aspect of the ≀   great toe measuring
approximately 1/2 cm in diameter.

NEUROLOGIC: Lethargic but arousable to voi≀   He states his name, location,
                  and the year with some difficu: He has no memory for the events
of the accident. Cranial nerves exam reveals pupils r   ⌐tive to light at 2 mm. EOMI.
Hearing appears normal. No facial asymmetry. Speech   ⌐al. Tongue protrudes in
midline. Sternocleidomastoid stre⌐gth good bilatrall⌐   Upper extremities reveal normal
motor strengths at biceps, triceps, and wrist dorsifle   ⌐n, finger-spread, and grip
strength bilaterally. Lower extremity motor exam reve   ⌐ he is able to elevate either leg
without difficulty, moves toes in dorsiflexion or pla⌐   ⌐flexion with good strength.
Sensory intact to light touch and pain throughout. R⌐   ⌐xes 1+ biceps, 1+ triceps, 2+
knees, 1+ ankle jerks, downgoing toes.   CT scan on a⌐   ⌐sion shows no acute intracranial
abnormality. One view of lateral c-spine has a quest⌐   ⌐ble area at left of C2-3 with
possibility of locked facet at this area. Chest x-ray   ⌐kull series, and extremity x-rays
appear normal to me.

IMPRESSION: 1. CLOSED HEAD INJURY WITH CON⌐   ⌐ION
                  2. POSSIBLE CERVICAL SPINE IN.

PLAN: Admit to Neuro ICU, obtain rou⌐   vital signs and neuro checks.
                  Keep in hard C-collar and obta⌐   . scan of area in question in the
neck in the morning.

WALTER BROWN, M.D.
EDWARD F. DOWNING, M. D.

WB:cwb
D: 8-24-86 22:31
T: 8-25-86 00:45

FORM 826.1

MEMORIAL MEDICAL CENTER, INC.
SAVANNAH, GEORGIA
DISCHARGE ORDER
Only the Completion of this Form
constitutes a Discharge Order

0455

DISCHARGE PATIENT (Date and Time) 8/26/86 @ 1²⁰/pm

238841-3   11/03/69
LEE, SHANE E   16 MM
LEESING EDWARD CERVICAL FR
FOR ADDRESSOGRAPH PLATE USE ONLY

PRINCIPAL DISCHARGE DIAGNOSIS FOR THIS ADMISSION

PRINCIPAL PROCEDURE AND/OR OPERATION FOR THIS ADMISSION

OTHER DISCHARGE DIAGNOSIS
1.
2.
3.

OTHER MAJOR PROCEDURES AND/OR OPERATIONS
1.
2.

DISCHARGE MEDICATIONS

N/A

SPECIAL INSTRUCTIONS TO PATIENT AT TIME OF DISCHARGE (Diet, instructions and/or recommendations for future care)
① May Shower
②

DISCHARGE TO:	APPOINTMENTS/REFERRALS		DISABILITY STATUS	
☒ Home	Doctor/Clinic	Date & Time	☐ Total _____ (duration)	
☐ Extended Care Facility	Dr. Downing Office	Sept. 3ʳᵈ 1986	☐ Partial _____ (duration)	
☐ Other Acute Facility		@ 10 am	☐ Return to Normal Duties	
☐ AMA			_____ (date)	

PHYSICIAN'S SIGNATURE Edward L. Downing M.D. DATE

Mode of discharge/transfer   RETURNED TO PATIENT: N/A
(   ) Stretcher (✓) Wheelchair   Medication (   )   Personal Items (   )
(   ) Ambulation (   ) Other   Clothing (   )
The above has been explained to me and I have had an opportunity to ask questions.

NURSE'S SIGNATURE _____

(mother)
Signature _____
Patient or Representative

DATE & TIME 8/26/86 @ 1²⁰/pm

MEDICAL RECORD

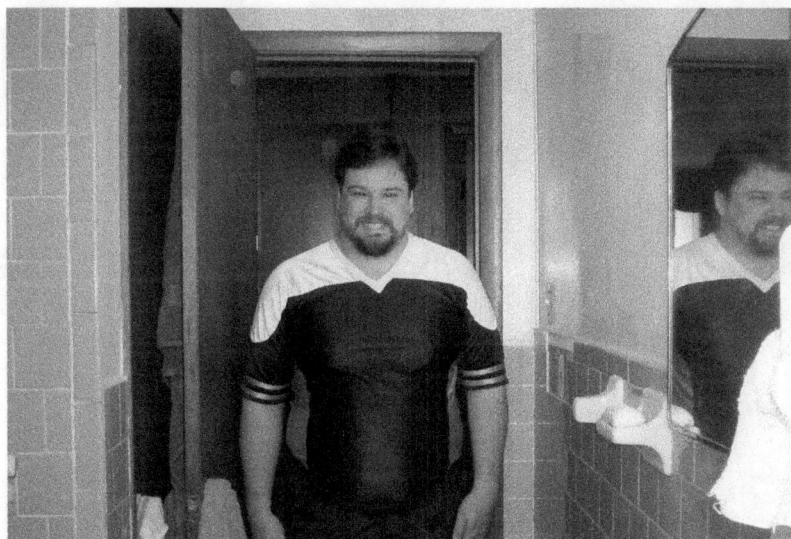

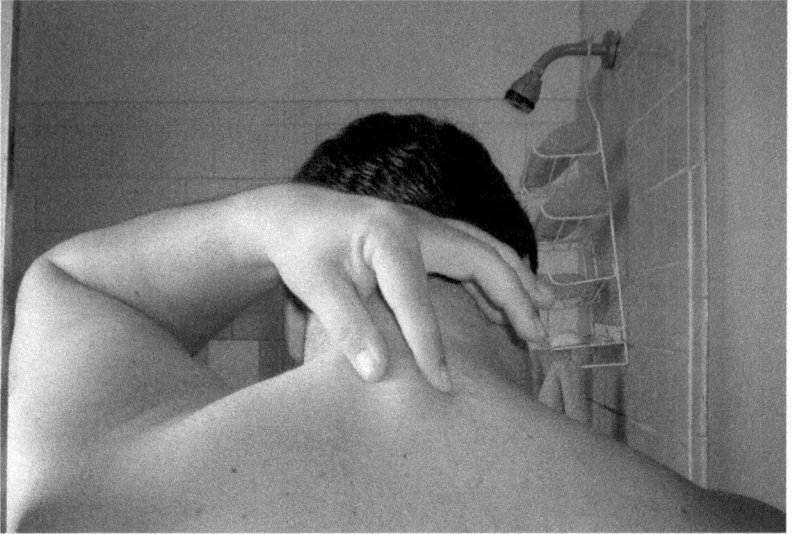

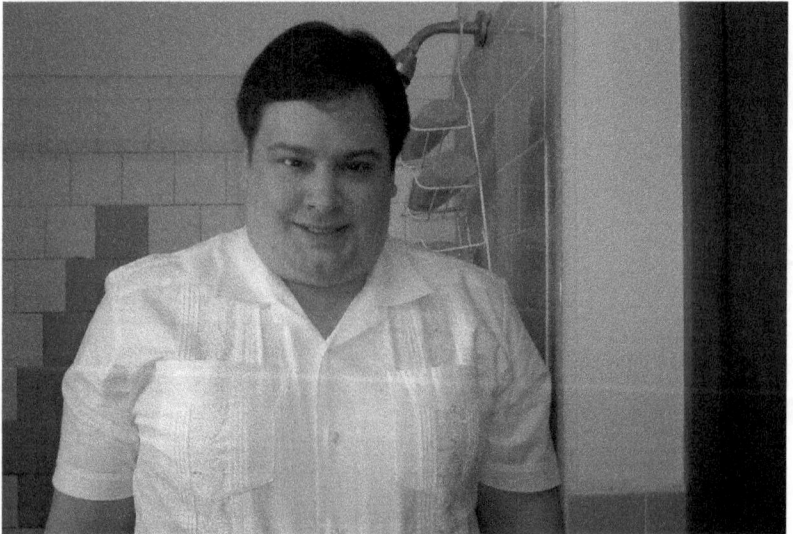

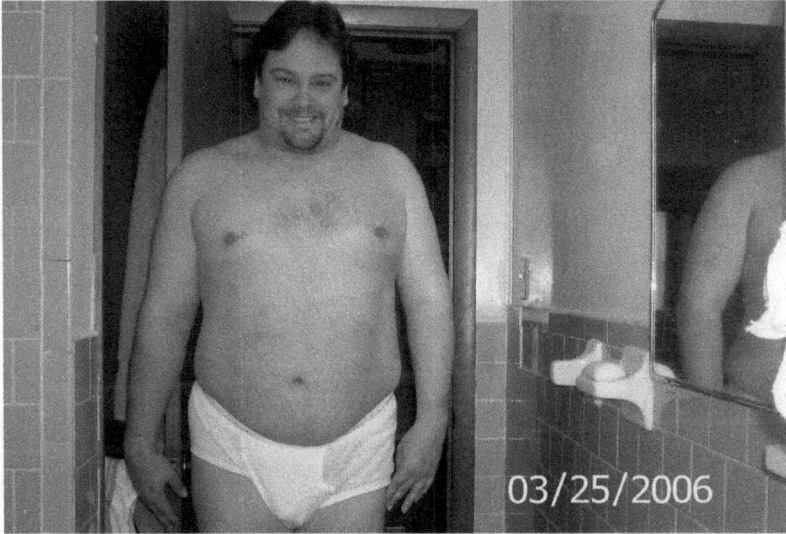

03/25/2006

DV 373E

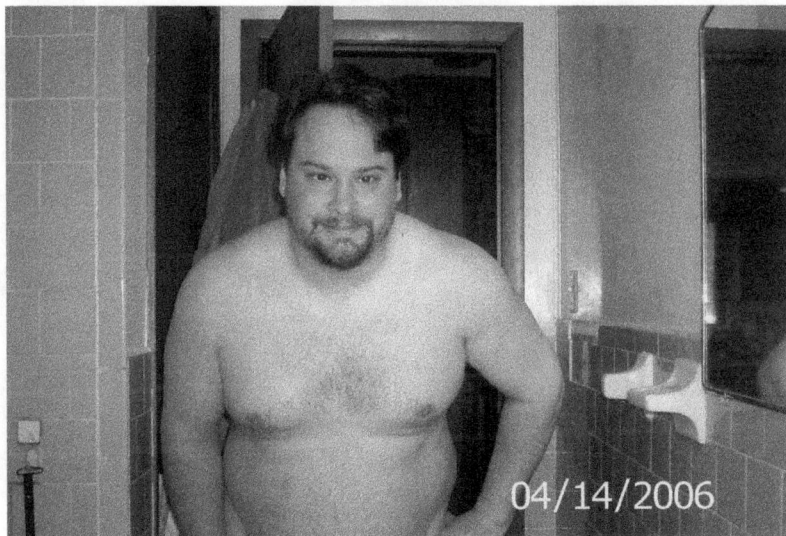

A GOOD BOOK

A GOOD BOOK

MEDICAL BOARD ADDENDUM ICO FA SHANE E. LEE, USN/███-██-████

MENTAL COMPETENCY: In accordance with the provisions of Chapter 15, JAG Manual, Paragraph 1504, staff psychiatrist concurs with the opinion of the previous board that the patient is mentally capable of handling his own financial affairs.

DISCIPLINARY STATUS: There is no known disciplinary action, investigation or processing for an administrative discharge pending at this time.

L. W. SLOAN   T. L. PORTER
LT, MC, USN   LCDR, MC, USNR
Psychiatry Resident   Staff Psychiatrist

I HAVE BEEN INFORMED OF THE CONTENTS, OPINIONS AND RECOMMENDATIONS OF THIS ADDENDUM AND I DO / DO NOT DESIRE TO SUBMIT A STATEMENT IN REBUTTAL.

_____
PT NAME

_____   _____
WITNESS   DATE

101

SHANE EDWARD LEE

5

12. MENTAL COMPETENCY: In accordance with the provisions of Chapter 15, JAG Manual, Paragraph 1504, the Board is of the opinion that the patient is mentally capable of handling his own financial affairs.

13. DISCIPLINARY STATUS: There is no known disciplinary action, investigation or processing for an administrative discharge pending.

M. J. OAKS (P)   S. AZNAR (P)   B. A. CAREY (P)
LT MC USNR   CDR MC USN   CAPT MC USN

LEE, SHANE E. ███-██-████   DOC. 6-6106   DATE: 1 DEC 93

A GOOD BOOK

NAVAL MEDICAL CENTER
PORTSMOUTH, VIRGINIA 23708-5100
REPORT OF MEDICAL BOARD
-SURREBUTTAL-

NAME: LEE, SHANE E..   RATE/RANK/SER: EMFA/USN/AD
SSN: 20 ███-██-████   TYPIST: SLB
DATE: 03 FEB 94.   DOC: 5-6529

The patient has been informed of the findings and the recommendations of the Board and does desire to submit a statement in rebuttal. Statement appended.

SURREBUTTAL: The Board has reviewed the member's rebuttal. The board submits the following for review:

1. With respect to the patient's assertion that his condition was aggravated by active duty, attention is directed to the history of present illness obtained from the patient, which refers to religious delusions and auditory hallucinations from the age of twelve years. It is clear from this history that a full schizophrenic break occurred during adolescence.

2. The patient's assertion that his delusions caused him no difficulty prior to entering the military, is taken as supporting evidence for the existence of the disorder prior to enlistment.

3. With respect to the patient's assertion that MCPI test given at the time of his sleep study evaluation failed to indicate a diagnosis of schizophrenia; test referred to is neither specific nor sufficient for diagnosis of schizophrenia.

4. With respect to the patient's assertion that he wrote a female shipmate 100 letters over a three to four month period rather than one month as stated, although the original time period was obtained from the patient's own history, this is not contested.

The findings and recommendations of the Board remain unchanged.

M. OAKS (P)
LT MC USNR
DICTATING PHYSICIAN

S. AZNAR (P)
CDR MC USN
ALTERNATE MEMBER

B. A. CAREY (P)
CAPT, MC, USN
SENIOR MEMBER

103

SHANE EDWARD LEE

NAVAL MEDICAL CENTER, PORTSMOUTH VIRGINIA
ADDENDUM TO REPORT OF MEDICAL BOARD

From: Medical Boards, Naval Medical Center, Portsmouth,
        Virginia 23708

To: Central Physical Evaluation Board, Naval Council
        Of Personnel Boards, Arlington, Virginia 22203

Via: Commanding Officer, Naval Medical Center, Portsmouth,
        Virginia, 23708

Subj: SA Shane E. LEE USNSSN: ██ █ ███; addendum to Report
        of Medical Board dated 1 Dec 93.

1.   The patient is a 24 year old active duty member who fell
three stories onto the pavement the day of admission. The
patient landed feet first and fell onto his left side. He was
admitted and cleared by General Surgery for his abdomen and
cervical spine. He was admitted to the Orthopedic Service with a
complaint of sacral and low back pain. The patient was diagnosed
with x-ray and physical examination to have a vertical shear
component complex pelvis fracture with elevation of the left
hemi-pelvis approximately .5 cm. to 1 cm. The patient also had a
large pelvic intraperitoneal hematoma which was stable. The
patient was taken to the operating room the day of admission
where he underwent closed reduction and placement of external
fixation device on his pelvis. Postoperative x-rays confirmed
maintenance of his reduction. He was admitted to the ward where
he was kept in a skeletal traction. It was noted during the
operation that the patient also had a left talar dome fracture
and lateral ligament disruption. The patient had an arthrotomy
performed, irrigation and debridement of the ankle joint, and
primary closure. The patient was placed into a short leg cast
postoperatively once the swelling went down and his splint was
removed. The patient was kept in skeletal traction for
approximately four weeks, and the traction was discharged after
x-rays were taken. One week post removal of the traction, the x-
rays were retaken and showed that there was minimal increase in
the change in the elevation of the pelvis. The patient was
undergoing bed to chair transfers, and at the point that the x-
rays were noted to be stable, he was progressed to toe-touch only
weightbearing on the left side. The patient had done well in
physical therapy with toe-touch weightbearing and it is planned
for him to be advanced to removal of the external fixation device
at the six to eight week point postoperatively. The patient will
be taken out of his short-leg cast at the six week point as well
and placed into a gel splint to allow range of motion exercises
and still maintain support to the lateral collateral ligaments.

LEE, SHANE E.   SSN: ██ ██   Page 1

104

MEDICAL RECORD	CONSULTATION SHEET

REQUEST

TO: *MHU.*   FROM: 237. BHAK   DATE: 20 AUG 1990

REASON FOR REQUEST:

20 y/o Caucasian male, FC/MAD. Unable to stay awake during day. Sleep well at night time. Lack of interest. No somatic complaints. Blood work-up WN. Please evaluate and advise.

Thank you.

PROVISIONAL DIAGNOSIS:

DOCTOR'S SIGNATURE: XANTHOPOULOS MD
XANT.JO-9455 GMO/STAFF

PLACE OF CONSULTATION: ☑ ON CALL   ☑ ROUTINE

CONSULTATION REPORT

O: This 20 y/o Caucasian male FR has reportedly been falling asleep in class at boot camp since joining the Navy 2/20/90, despite getting a good night's sleep. In the past, particularly in high school, member would fall asleep in an early A.M. class if he had not gotten a full night's sleep due to staying up too late. He was also fired from a job 2 or day due to falling asleep again in an early AM assignment. At this time he sleeps 6-8 hrs/nite & denied all depression Sxs. He stated that he falls asleep both in school & on watch at least 4x/day for 10-15 mins. Standing up doesn't prevent his falling asleep. Member states his Fr. had this problem & was seen by family members as "lazy." Member has had 2 head traumas: at age 17 he was in a car accident in which he was reportedly unconscious for 3 days & still has amnesia for the actual collision; at age 18 he was hit by a car while riding his bicycle, flew over the handlebars and landed head on the car. He says an ambulance driver told him he had a slight concussion, but did not receive ER treatment. He was probably dizzy following this event. Member has reportedly had 2 car accidents due to falling asleep at the wheel.

MSE was WNL. No suicidal or homicidal thoughts, plans or intent. Past hx reveals parents' divorce when he was 13, & mo. remarrying when he was 9. Reports close/positive relationships & all caretakers

SIGNATURE: Weinrep, Psy.D.

ANNE WEINREP, PSY.D.
364-42-6098
CLINICAL PSYCHOLOGIST

DATE: 8/2 9/90

IDENTIFICATION NO.   ORGANIZATION: MHU   WARD NO: 68-200H

PATIENT'S IDENTIFICATION: LEF. TRIMP

STANDARD FORM 513 (Rev. 9-77)

member has been extremely religious since age 9 & act
proselytizing. Mayorly identified as being a Christian. Re
3rd grade as a slow learner; failed 11th grade due to staying
late; not studying & falling asleep in class. He quit there
Had 75-80 GPA in high school & sports & studies. Had church &
Job hx is for short periods & 1 firing due to sleep problem. Had
an accomplice to a burglary & brothers friends to receive
~ 200 community service hrs (waived by Navy). No other a
hx- Alcohol use consisted of 1 beer at age 13 and 3 beers a
rarely gets angry.

A. This interview does not explain causation of sleep prob
Further data is needed & will be obtained
Axis I - Hypersomnia, cause of which is currently unknown
member is psychological fit for Naval duty, pending of
evaluation & Rx.
P. ① member to get data from mp. re dad's sleep disor
② member to chart data re: his hypersomnia (e) -
where, how long etc) to get more complete data. ③ a
referral to Neurology will be made to R/O organic
④ member will be taught ways to cope & this prob
not organic.

Psychological Testing
a member was given mcmI to aid in evaluation. I
valid. It showed some mild anxiety, depression & high
personality profile shows someone who is perfectio
and inflexible and uses considerable structure &
anxiety.

A GOOD BOOK

DATE	SYMPTOMS, DIAGNOSIS, TREATMENT, TREATING ORGANIZATION (Sign each entry)	
9/12/90	8:00 – 8:20	20 min
	9:00 – 9:10	10 min
	9:50 – 10:05	15 min
	10:35 – 10:50	15 min
	1:05 – 1:10	5 min
	1:40 – 1:55	15 min
9/13/90	9:10 – 9:20	10 min
	9:25 – 9:55	20 min
	10:20 – 10:30	10 min
	10:35 – 10:40	5 min
	12:15 – 12:25	10 min
	1:25 – 1:35	10 min
	1:50 – 2:00	10 min

NO FURTHER ENTRIES THIS PAGE

MEDICAL RECORD	CONSULTATION

REQUEST

FROM:

Neurology

[Reason for request — handwritten, largely illegible] This is a 20 y.o. Caucasian male ... falling asleep in class & during ... thought he gets a full night's sleep. Hx of ... age ... 2nd day to car accident & amnesia for ... age 18 landed head ... on a car hood in a bicycle ... evaluate whether an organic cause exists for the acknowledged depressive disorders 5 ...

PROVISIONAL DIAGNOSIS
Hypersomnia

DOCTOR'S SIGNATURE
ANNE WEINREP, PSY.D.
364-42-6098
CLINICAL PSYCHOLOGIST

APPROVED

PLACE OF CONSULTATION
☐ BEDSIDE ☒ ON CALL

CONSULTATION REPORT

[Handwritten consultation notes — largely illegible]

14 SEP 70 Dr. Gaffney

20 y.o. RH ♂ ... hypersomnolence ... work after ... feels tired all the time; falls asleep early at class, & driving. Occurred in high school, work after accident, in a lot of classes; ... as well, as fueled 11 hrs. Sleeps longer on weekends but doesn't really help. ... or sleep related hallucinations. No clear Pt ... father "slept a lot"; died of "gunshot wound" when Pt ... No snoring or Am HA; but Pt gets frequent HA per week, lasts a few hrs; occipital & throbbing. HA have been a problem since MVA. MVA result ... hospitalization, "unconscious" x 3 days (?) ⊖ ETOH, tobacco ...

(Continued on reverse side)

SIGNATURE AND TITLE
J GAFFNEY M.D.
LCDR, MC, USNR
GAFFJA-2560
NEUROLOGY STAFF

IDENTIFICATION NO.   ORGANIZATION

PATIENT'S IDENTIFICATION
Lee, Shane

2. DIAGNOSES: 1. COMPLEX PELVIS FRACTURE WITH VERTICAL SHEAR
COMPONENT OF THE LEFT HEMI-PELVIS, #8088
2. GRADE III ANKLE SPRAIN WITH OSTEOCHONDRAL
DEFECT OF THE TALAR DOME, #84500, #7388

3. It is the opinion of the Medical Board that the member's
medical condition interferes with the reasonable performance of
assigned duties. On that basis, this case is referred to the
Physical Evaluation Board for fitness for duty determination.

4. It is recommended that pending disposition that the patient
continue with his inpatient care and progress toward outpatient
care which he will be able to continue through the VA system.

BRYAN HERRON
LCMC USNR

MARTIN A. DEFENBAUGH
CAPT MC USN

I HAVE READ THE CONTENTS OF THE ADDENDUM AND I DO/DO NOT DESIRE
TO SUBMIT A STATEMENT IN REBUTTAL.

Shane E. Lee
PT. NAME   RANK

Cindy Thenier   11/3/94
WITNESS   DATE

FIRST ENDORSEMENT   Code 3095/PJH

From: Commanding Officer, Naval Medical Center, Portsmouth,
       Virginia 23708
To: Central Physical Evaluation Board, Naval Council of
       Personnel Boards, Arlington, Virginia 22203

1. Forwarded.

                              K. BUCHTA
                              By direction

D: 24 OCT 1994   T: 24 OCT 1994   D-PJH3886/3732

LEE, SHANE E.   SSN: ██ █ ████   Page 2

SHANE EDWARD LEE

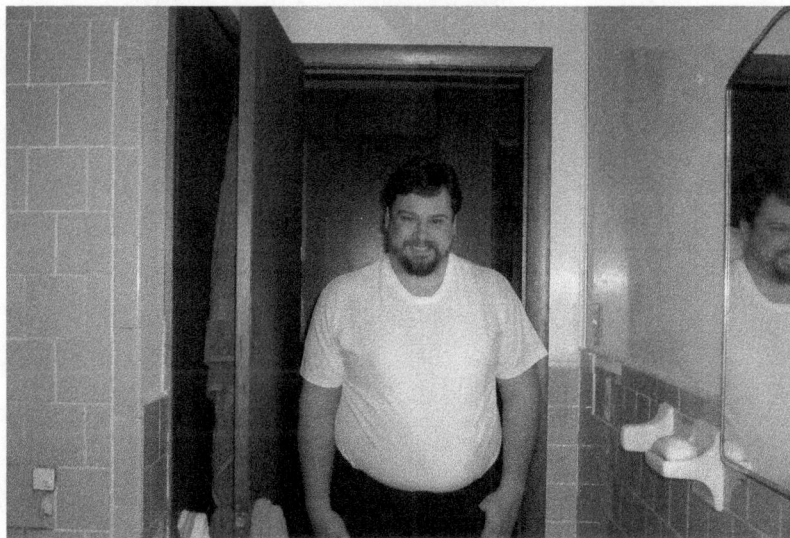

A GOOD BOOK

504

REVELATION XII.6—XIII.1

the dragon stood before the woman which was ready to be delivered, for to devour her child as soon as it was born.

5 And she brought forth a man child, who was to rule all nations with a rod of iron:¹ and her child was caught up unto God, and to his throne.²

6 And the woman fled into the wilderness, where she hath a place prepared of God, that they should feed her there a thousand two hundred and threescore days.

7 And there was war in heaven: Michael and his angels fought against the dragon; and the dragon fought and his angels,

8 And prevailed not; neither was their place found any more in heaven.

9 And the great dragon was cast out, that old serpent, called the Devil, and Satan, which deceiveth the whole world: he was cast out into the earth, and his angels were cast out with him.

10 And I heard a loud voice saying in heaven, Now is come salvation, and strength, and the kingdom of our God, and the power of his Christ: for the accuser of our brethren is cast down, which accused them before our God day and night.

11 And they overcame him by the blood of the Lamb, and by the word of their testimony; and they loved not their lives unto the death.

12 Therefore rejoice, ye heavens, and ye that dwell in them. Woe to the inhabiters of the earth and of the sea! for the devil is come down unto you, having great wrath, because he knoweth that he hath but a short time.

13 And when the dragon saw that he was cast unto the earth, he persecuted the woman which brought forth the man child.

14 And to the woman were given two wings of a great eagle, that she might fly into the wilderness, into her place, where she is nourished for a time, and times, and half a time, from the face of the serpent.

15 And the serpent cast out of his mouth water as a flood after the woman, that he might cause her to be carried away of the flood.

16 And the earth helped the woman, and the earth opened her mouth, and swallowed up the flood which the dragon cast out of his mouth.

17 And the dragon was wroth with the woman, and went to make war with the remnant of her seed, which keep the commandments of God, and have the testimony of Jesus Christ.

XIII And I stood upon the sand of the sea, and saw a beast rise up out of the sea, having seven heads and ten horns, and upon his horns ten crowns, and upon his

¹ Psalm 2. 8, 9.   ² Psalm 110. 1.

חזיון XII.5—XIII.1   504

5 וַתֵּלֶד בֵּן זָכָר אֲשֶׁר עָתִיד לִרְעוֹת אֶת־כָּל־הַגּוֹיִם בְּשֵׁבֶט בַּרְזֶל וַיִּלָּקַח בְּנָהּ אֶל־הָאֱלֹהִים וְאֶל־כִּסְאוֹ׃

6 וְהָאִשָּׁה בָּרְחָה הַמִּדְבָּרָה אֲשֶׁר שָׁם מְכוֹן לָהּ עַל־פִּי הָאֱלֹהִים לְכַלְכֵּל אֹתָהּ שָׁם יָמִים אֶלֶף וּמָאתַיִם וְשִׁשִּׁים׃

7 וַתְּהִי מִלְחָמָה בַּשָּׁמַיִם מִיכָאֵל וּמַלְאָכָיו נִלְחֲמוּ עִם־הַתַּנִּין וְהַתַּנִּין וּצְבָאָיו נִלְחֲמוּ קָרָב׃

8 וְלֹא כָּלְלוּ לָהֶם וּמְקוֹמָם לֹא נִמְצָא עוֹד בַּשָּׁמָיִם׃

9 וַיֻּשְׁלַךְ הַתַּנִּין הַגָּדוֹל הוּא הַנָּחָשׁ הַקַּדְמוֹנִי אֲשֶׁר קָרְאוּ לוֹ שָׂטָן וְרָשָׁע אֲשֶׁר הִדִּיחַ עָלֵי־יֵשְׁבֵי תֵבֵל אֹתוֹ

10 וְאֶת־מַלְאָכָיו עִמּוֹ הֻשְׁלִיכוּ אָרְצָה וָאֶשְׁמַע קוֹל גָּדוֹל בַּשָּׁמַיִם לֵאמֹר הַיּוֹם בָּאָה יְשׁוּעַת אֱלֹהֵינוּ גְּבוּרָתוֹ וּמַלְכוּתוֹ וּמֶמְשֶׁלֶת מְשִׁיחוֹ כִּי־הוּרַד שׂוֹטֵן אַחֵינוּ

11 אֲשֶׁר־עָמַד לְשִׂטְנָם לִפְנֵי אֱלֹהֵינוּ יוֹמָם וָלָיְלָה׃ וְהֵם גָּבְרוּ עָלָיו בְּדַם הַשֶּׂה וּבַעֲבוּר פִּיהֶם וְלֹא אָהֲבוּ

12 אֶת־נַפְשָׁם עַד־מָוֶת׃ עַל־כֵּן רָנּוּ שָׁמַיִם וְצָגְלוּ אַתֶּם הַשּׁוֹכְנִים שָׁם אוֹי לְיֹשְׁבֵי הָאָרֶץ וּלְשׁוֹכְנֵי הַיָּם כִּי־יָרַד אֲלֵיכֶם הַשָּׂטָן וַחֲמָתוֹ גְדוֹלָה כִּי מַדַּעְתּוֹ כִּי תִקְצַר עִתּוֹ׃

13 וַיִּרְאֶה הַתַּנִּין כִּי הוּרַד אָרְצָה וַיִּרְדֹּף אַחֲרֵי הָאִשָּׁה

14 אֲשֶׁר יָלְדָה אֶת בֵּן הַזָּכָר׃ וַיִּתְּנוּ לָאִשָּׁה שְׁתֵּי כַנְפֵי הַנֶּשֶׁר הַגָּדוֹל לָעוּף הַמִּדְבָּרָה אֶל־הַמָּקוֹם אֲשֶׁר

15 יְכַלְכְּלוּ אֹתָהּ מוֹעֵד מוֹעֲדִים וַחֲצִי מִפְּנֵי הַנָּחָשׁ׃ וַיָּקֶא הַנָּחָשׁ נָהָר־מַיִם מִפִּיו אַחֲרֵי הָאִשָּׁה לִשְׁטֹף אוֹתָהּ בַּנָּהָר׃

16 וַתַּעֲזֹר הָאָרֶץ לָאִשָּׁה וַתִּפְתַּח הָאָרֶץ אֶת־פִּיהָ וַתִּבְלַע אֶת־הַנָּהָר אֲשֶׁר־הֵקִיא הַתַּנִּין מִפִּיו׃

17 וַיִּקְצֹף הַתַּנִּין עַל־הָאִשָּׁה וַיֵּלֶךְ לְהִלָּחֵם בְּיֶתֶר זַרְעָהּ שֹׁמְרֵי מִצְוֹת

XIII אֱלֹהִים וַעֲדוּת יֵשׁוּעַ אֹתָם׃ וָאֶעֱמֹד עַל־חוֹל שְׂפַת הַיָּם וָאֵרֶא חַיָּה עֹלָה מִדַּרַיִּם אֲשֶׁר לָהּ שִׁבְעָה רָאשִׁים וְעֶשֶׂר קְרָנָיִם וְעַל־קַרְנֶיהָ עֶשֶׂר עֲטָרוֹת וּשְׁמוֹת גְּדוּפִים

REVELATION 10.8–11.10

the voice of the seventh angel, when he shall begin to sound, the mystery of God should be finished, as he hath declared to his servants the prophets.

8 And the voice which I heard from heaven spake unto me again, and said, Go and take the little book which is open in the hand of the angel which standeth upon the sea and upon the earth.

9 And I went unto the angel, and said unto him, Give me the little book. And he said unto me, Take it, and eat it up; and it shall make thy belly bitter, but it shall be in thy mouth sweet as honey.

10 And I took the little book out of the angel's hand, and ate it up; and it was in my mouth sweet as honey: and as soon as I had eaten it, my belly was bitter.

11 And he said unto me, Thou must prophesy again before many peoples, and nations, and tongues, and kings.

XI And there was given me a reed like unto a rod: and the angel stood, saying, Rise, and measure the temple of God, and the altar, and them that worship therein.

2 But the court which is without the temple leave out, and measure it not; for it is given unto the Gentiles: and the holy city shall they tread under foot forty and two months.

3 And I will give power unto my two witnesses, and they shall prophesy a thousand two hundred and threescore days, clothed in sackcloth.

4 These are the two olive trees, and the two candlesticks standing before the God of the earth.

5 And if any man will hurt them, fire proceedeth out of their mouth, and devoureth their enemies: and if any man will hurt them, he must in this manner be killed.

6 These have power to shut heaven, that it rain not in the days of their prophecy: and have power over waters to turn them to blood, and to smite the earth with all plagues, as often as they will.

7 And when they shall have finished their testimony, the beast that ascendeth out of the bottomless pit shall make war against them, and shall overcome them, and kill them.

8 And their dead bodies shall lie in the street of the great city, which spiritually is called Sodom and Egypt, where also our Lord was crucified.

9 And they of the people and kindreds and tongues and nations shall see their dead bodies three days and an half, and shall not suffer their dead bodies to be put in graves.

10 And they that dwell upon the earth shall rejoice

A GOOD BOOK

113

NAME: LEE, SHANE

AGE: 16 SEX: WM RACE:

X-RAY NO: 238841-3

HOSP/OPD NO: I/O: _____

RADIOLOGY ASSOCIATES OF SAVANNAH, P.A.

DEPARTMENT OF RADIOLOGY

MEMORIAL MEDICAL CENTER, INC.

Savannah, Georgia

Date 8/25/86

DR. DOWNING
4 JACKSON BLVD.
SAVANNAH, GA. 31405

466

EXAMINATION
LEFT SHOULDER

Medicare _____ Medicaid _____

REPORT OF RADIOLOGIC EXAMINATION

15

HX: MVA.

LEFT SHOULDER:

The bony structures demonstrate no evidence of fracture or other significant abnormality.

William A. Miller, M.D./jr M.D.
Radiologist

A.C.R. NO: _____
ADDITIONAL INFORMATION FOR CODING:

LEE, SHANE   ORIGINAL

SHANE EDWARD LEE

NAME: LEE, SHANE
AGE: 16 SEX: M RACE:
X-RAY NO: 238841-3
HOSPIOPD NO: I/O:

RADIOLOGY ASSOCIATES OF SAVANNAH, P.A.
DEPARTMENT OF RADIOLOGY
MEMORIAL MEDICAL CENTER, INC.
Savannah, Georgia

Date 8-25-86

DR. EDWARD DOWNING
4 JACKSON BLVD.
SAVANNAH, GA. 31405

EXAMINATION
CT OF SCAN OF THE
CERVICAL SPINE

Medicare _____ Medicaid _____

REPORT OF RADIOLOGIC EXAMINATION

54
HX: MVA - R/O C2-C3 locked facet

CT SCAN OF THE CERVICAL SPINE: CT scan of the cervcial spine was performed
extending from the C2 vertebral body to the superior aspect of the C4 vertebral
body. There is no evidence of a fracture or locked facet. No other
abnormality is identified.

OPINION:
No evidence of a fracture or locked facet with specific attention to the C2-3
level.

TERRY L. REYNOLDS, M.D./oc
Radiologist

A.G.R. NO: _____
ADDITIONAL INFORMATION FOR CODING:

ORIGINAL

116

A GOOD BOOK

NAME: LEE, SHANE

AGE: 16 SEX: M RACE:

X-RAY NO: 238841-3

HOSP/OPD NO: I/O:

RADIOLOGY ASSOCIATES OF SAVANNAH, P.A.

DEPARTMENT OF RADIOLOGY

MEMORIAL MEDICAL CENTER, INC.

Savannah, Georgia

-ER/IC

Date 8-25-86

DR. EDWARD DOWNING
4 JACKSON BLVD.
SAVANNAH, GA. 31405

EXAMINATION
CT OF SCAN OF THE
BRAIN

Medicare _____ Medicaid _____

REPORT OF RADIOLOGIC EXAMINATION

54
HX: MVA

CT BRAIN SCAN: A CT brain scan was performed without contrast enhancement.
There is asymmetry of the frontal horns of the lateral ventricles which is
probably related to normal variation. There is no evidence of midline shift.
There is no evidence of intracranial hemorrhage. No abnormal areas of
increased or decreased attenuation are evident.

OPINION:
Asymmetry of the frontal horns of the lateral ventricles which is most likely
normal variation. The remainder of the CT brain scan is unremarkable.

_____ TERRY L. REYNOLDS, M.D. /nc M.D.
Radiologist

A.O.R. NO: _____
ADDITIONAL INFORMATION FOR CODING:

ORIGINAL

117

NAME: LEE, SHANE	**RADIOLOGY ASSOCIATES OF SAVANNAH, P.A.**
AGE: 16 SEX: M RACE:	DEPARTMENT OF RADIOLOGY
X-RAY NO: 238841-3	**MEMORIAL MEDICAL CENTER, INC.**
HOSP/OPD NO: I/O:	Savannah, Georgia

ER/NIC   Date 8-25-86

DR. EDWARD DOWNING
4 JACKSON BLVD.
SAVANNAH, GA. 31405

EXAMINATION
CT OF SCAN OF THE
BRAIN

Medicare _____ Medicaid _____

REPORT OF RADIOLOGIC EXAMINATION

54
HX: MVA

CT BRAIN SCAN: A CT brain scan was performed without contrast enhancement.
There is asymmetry of the frontal horns of the lateral ventricles which is
probably related to normal variation. There is no evidence of midline shift.
There is no evidence of intracranial hemorrhage. No abnormal areas of
increased or decreased attenuation are evident.

OPINION:
Asymmetry of the frontal horns of the lateral ventricles which is most likely
normal variation. The remainder of the CT brain scan is unremarkable.

Terry L. Reynolds

TERRY L. REYNOLDS, M.D./nc   M.D.
Radiologist

A.C.R. NO: _____
ADDITIONAL INFORMATION FOR CODING:

ORIGINAL

A GOOD BOOK

NAME: LEE, SHANE

AGE: 16 SEX: M RACE: W

X-RAY NO: 238841-3

HOSP/OPO NO: I/O: _____

DR. MARTIN

RADIOLOGY ASSOCIATES OF SAVANNAH, P.A.

DEPARTMENT OF RADIOLOGY

MEMORIAL MEDICAL CENTER, INC.

Savannah, Georgia

ER   Date 8/23/86

EXAMINATION
MULTIPLE EXAMS

Medicare _____ Medicaid _____

REPORT OF RADIOLOGIC EXAMINATION

02

HX: MVA - MULTIPLE INJURIES

SKULL: The bones of the calvarium and base of the skull appear intact. The sella turcica is of normal size and configuration. There are no abnormal intracranial calcifications.

CERVICAL SPINE: The vertebral bodies, interspaces, spinous processes and lateral masses are all within normal limits. The neural foramina are patent.

RIGHT FOOT: The bony structures demonstrate no evidence of fracture or other significant abnormality.

RIGHT FEMUR: The bony structures demonstrate no evidence of fracture or other significant abnormality.

RIGHT HAND: Small radiopaque densities on the dorsum of the hand at the level of the wrist are observed, presumably some radiopaque material secondary to injury. I recognize no air within the deep soft tissues nor in the joints identified. No fractures or subluxations on examination of the right hand are apparent.

CHEST: A single AP supine view of the chest is submitted and shows the lung fields to be clear. No infiltrates or effusions are apparent. No pneumothorax is observed. The heart and mediastinal structures are unremarkable and the bony thorax is grossly intact.

A.C.R. NO: _____

ADDITIONAL INFORMATION FOR CODING:

Radiologist _____ M.D.

Robert F. Long, M.D./jr

ORIGINAL

119

SHANE EDWARD LEE

DOI Sept 94
fell 3 stories
① vertical shear pelvic
② Ⓛ talar dome fx

EXAM: tender over anterior
lat/medial talar dome
Ⓛ ankle c/w old
intraarticular fx
ROM 10° DF
25° PF

Ⓐ s/p fall
① healed vertical shear pelvic fx
② s/p talar dome fx
Ⓟ PBS pending

FRANCIS M. SWEENEY
CDR MC USNR
ORTHOPEDIC SURGERY
104 460-96-8750

120

A GOOD BOOK

DENTAL HEALTH QUESTIONNAIRE — Personal Data - Privacy Act of 1974 — NAVMEDCOMINST 6600.3

INSTRUCTIONS: Please answer the following questions by circling, and if applicable by entering the appropriate response.

ARE YOU IN: FLIGHT STATUS? . . . YES (NO) / PERSONNEL RELIABILITY PROGRAM? . . . YES (NO)
ARE YOU PRESENTLY ILL OR UNDER THE CARE OF A PHYSICIAN? . . . . YES (NO)

IF YES, PLEASE DESCRIBE:
HISTORY OF HOSPITALIZATIONS: _COUNSLES_ _EYE SURGARY_ _CAR ACCIDENT_

ANY ALLERGIES? _NONE_
MEDICATIONS PRESENTLY TAKING: _NONE_
(Including aspirin, etc.)

ANY FAMILY HISTORY OF: (Circle)
Heart Disease — ~~Cancer~~
Diabetes — Seizures NONE

YOUR SOCIAL HISTORY: Occupation/Jobs: _SR_
- Type and frequency of:
- Tobacco use: _NONE_
- Alcohol consumption: _1 Every 8 month_

HAVE YOU EVER HAD OR OR HAVE YOU NOW: *(Please check at the RIGHT of each item)*

(check each item)	YES	NO	DON'T KNOW	(check each item)	YES	NO	DON'T KNOW	(check each item)	YES	NO	DON'T KNOW
Epilepsy or Seizures		/		Hemophilia			/	Ulcers		/	
Fainting or Dizziness		/		Bruise or bleed easily			/	Kidney problems		/	
Nervousness		/		Heart problems or Angina			/	Venereal disease		/	
Stroke		/		Hypertension			/	Diabetes		/	
Glaucoma		/		Rheumatic fever			/	Thyroid disease		/	
Cold sores (Herpes)		/		Heart murmur			/	AIDS/HTLV-III positive		/	
Persistent cough		/		Mitral valve prolapse			/	Arthritis		/	
Emphysema		/		Congenital heart lesions			/	Painful joints (incl. jaw)		/	
Tuberculosis/PPD positive		/		Heart surgery			/	Prosthetic joint(s)		/	
Asthma		/		Prosthetic heart valve(s)			/	Hives		/	
Hay fever		/		Pacemaker			/	Steroid medication(s)		/	
Sinus problems _OK_		/		Blood transfusion(s)			/	Drug addiction		/	
Anemia		/		Liver disease			/	Alcoholism		/	
Sickle cell disease		/		Yellow jaundice			/	Unexplained weight change		/	
G-6PD deficiency		/		Hepatitis- type:			/	Cancer/radiation therapy		/	

1. HAVE YOU EVER BEEN TOLD THAT YOU SHOULD NOT DONATE BLOOD? . . . .

2. FEMALES: Are you taking birth control pills (BCPs)? . . . .
   Are you or might you be pregnant? (Estimated delivery_____)

3. DO YOU HAVE ANY DISEASE, CONDITION, OR PROBLEM NOT LISTED ABOVE? . . . . .
   - IF YES, PLEASE DESCRIBE: _____

SUMMARY OF PERTINENT FINDINGS / RECOMMENDED TREATMENT MODIFICATIONS: *(Dentist's use only)*

(Continue on reverse)

Patient's Signature: _Shane E Lee_ — Date: _01MAR99_
Dental Officer's Signature: GRANKEE, R.J. LT, DC, USNR — Date: MAR 0 1 199?

PATIENT'S IDENTIFICATION *(Use this space for Mechanical Imprint)*

PATIENT'S NAME *(Last, First, Middle Initial)*: _Lee, Shane E_ — SEX: M

DATE OF BIRTH: _01 NOV 69_ — RELATIONSHIP TO SPONSOR: — COMPONENT/STATUS: _USN_ — DEPARTMENT/SERVICE: _DCD_
SPONSOR'S NAME: — RANK/GRADE: _SR_

SSN OR IDENTIFICATION NO: — ORGANIZATION:

SHANE EDWARD LEE

DIV: NH PO {MOUTH.VA
Automated Version of SF600

C PNH
27 Dec 1994 8:09 AM   ROU   8HBA

F: Recover from fall 2 mos ago
CMT: ROU

N: NEED LIGHT LIMIT DUTY CHIT
FLIGHT STATUS? Y or (N)

ME: HIV: TET: LMF:
TOBACCO USER? Y or (N)

:13?/82 PULSE: 100   RESP: 16   TEMP: 97.4   HT: 68"   WT: 170   AGE: 25

lergies: Yes (No) | Meds: Yes (No) | Orders: | Init | Time

| | | | ACH | 0815 |

walk-in

ditional Comments:

① 25 yo wm s/p pelvic fx Sept 94, awaiting PEB in Med Hold. Last seen by Ortho 16 Dec 94, did not address current duty status.

② It limiting the leg brace w/ crutches

③ s/p pelvic fx, awaiting PEB

④ Light duty as per dut works

F/U w/ Ortho in Portsmouth

RC Fenton LT MC
800 74 8685

/▓▓▓-▓▓-▓▓▓▓ LEE.SHANE E   N11
             03 NOV 1969 MALE   W: 804-398-7525   H: 804-397-1037
             Spon: LEE.SHANE E   CIC:

A GOOD BOOK

DEPARTMENT OF VETERANS AFFAIRS
ATLANTA VA REGIONAL OFFICE
PO BOX 100021
DECATUR GA 30031-7021

Shane E. Lee

VA File Number
257 23 2433

Represented by:
GEORGIA DEPARTMENT OF VETERAN SERVICE

Rating Decision
April 11, 2005

INTRODUCTION

The records reflect that you are a veteran of the Peacetime and Gulf War Era. You served in the Navy from February 20, 1990 to August 20, 1995. You filed a new claim for benefits that was received on March 25, 2004. Based on a review of the evidence listed below, we have made the following decision(s) on your claim.

DECISION

1 . Service connection for right eye vision loss is denied.

2 . Service connection for low back condition is denied.

3 . Service connection for coccyx injury is denied.

4 . Service connection for post-traumatic stress disorder (PTSD) is denied.

5 . Entitlement to an earlier effective date for the 100 percent evaluation of paranoid schizophrenia is denied.

Shane E. Lee
257 23 2433
Page 2

EVIDENCE

- Service medical records from August 29, 1989 (entrance examination) to March, 1995
- Treatment reports from Memorial Medical Center from May, 1998
- Treatment reports from VAMC, Charleston from November, 2000 to February, 2004
- DD Form 214

REASONS FOR DECISION

1. Service connection for right eye vision loss.

The service medical records were reviewed and showed that you reported having eye surgery when you were ten years old, however, your corrected vision appeared to be 20/20. No vision loss was noted in the private treatment reports or VA treatment reports.

Service connection may be granted for a disability which began in military service or was caused by some event or experience in service. Service connection for right eye vision loss is denied since this condition neither occurred in nor was caused by service.

2. Service connection for low back condition.

The service medical records were reviewed and showed treatment in June, 1991 for a low back muscle strain. This condition resolved with treatment. In November, 1993 you fell three stories to the pavement and injured your pelvis and left ankle. You then complained of having some low back pain but no diagnosed disability was shown. No subsequent treatment for a back condition was shown. The VA treatment reports showed that you complained of having back pain in November, 2002 but no diagnosis was provided.

Service connection may be granted for a disability which began in military service or was caused by some event or experience in service.

A disability which began in service or was caused by some event in service must be considered "chronic" before service connection can be granted. Although there is a record of treatment in service for low back condition, no permanent residual or chronic disability subject to service connection is shown by the service medical records or demonstrated by evidence following service. Therefore, service connection for low back condition is denied.

3. Service connection for coccyx injury.

A GOOD BOOK

Shane E. Lee
257 23 2433
Page 3

The service medical records were reviewed and showed that while you had a fall in 1993 there was no indication that you injured your coccyx at that time. The private treatment reports and VA treatment reports showed no evidence of treatment for a coccyx injury.

Service connection may be granted for a disability which began in military service or was caused by some event or experience in service. Service connection for coccyx injury is denied since this condition neither occurred in nor was caused by service.

4. Service connection for post-traumatic stress disorder.

There was no indication in your DD Form 214 that you were awarded a combat decoration. There was no indication in your service medical records of treatment for sexual abuse. You are currently service connected for paranoid schizophrenia. The private treatment reports and VA treatment reports showed treatment for paranoid schizophrenia with no indication of a diagnosis of PTSD.

Service connection for post-traumatic stress disorder requires medical evidence diagnosing the condition in accordance with 38 CFR 4.125(a); a link, established by medical evidence, between current symptoms and an in-service stressor; and credible supporting evidence that the claimed in-service stressor occurred. If the evidence establishes that the veteran engaged in combat with the enemy and the claimed stressor is related to that combat, in the absence of clear and convincing evidence to the contrary, and provided that the claimed stressor is consistent with the circumstances, conditions, or hardships of the veteran's service, occurrence of the claimed in-service stressor may be established by the veteran's lay testimony alone. If the evidence establishes that the veteran was a prisoner-of-war under the provisions of 38 CFR 3.1(y) and the claimed stressor is related to that prisoner-of-war experience, in the absence of clear and convincing evidence to the contrary, and provided that the claimed stressor is consistent with the circumstances, conditions, or hardships of the veteran's service, occurrence of the claimed in-service stressor may be established by the veteran's lay testimony alone. {38 CFR Sections 3.1(y), 3.304(f), 4.125(a)}

The available evidence is insufficient to confirm that the veteran actually engaged in combat or was a prisoner of war.

A diagnosis of post-traumatic stress disorder must meet all diagnostic criteria as stated in the Diagnostic and Statistical Manual of Mental Disorders published by the American Psychiatric Association. The evidence does not show a confirmed diagnosis of post-traumatic stress disorder which would permit a finding of service connection.

5. Entitlement to an earlier effective date for the evaluation assigned to the service connected paranoid schizophrenia.

SHANE EDWARD LEE

You requested that an earlier effective be granted for the award of a 100 percent disability evaluation for your service connected paranoid schizophrenia. A review of your claims folder showed that you were awarded a 10 percent disability effective from August 21, 1995 the day after your discharge from military service. A VA examination was scheduled for you but you failed to report for that examination. Your 10 percent disability evaluation was based on the evidence of record which consisted of your service medical records. You were informed of that decision on May 7, 1996. You had one year from that date to file an appeal. You failed to file an appeal within the one year time period so that decision became final. You reopened your claim for benefits on November 21, 1997 and eventually reported for a scheduled VA examination. Based on the evidence of record which included the VA examination, it was determined that you should be awarded a 100 percent disability evaluation for paranoid schizophrenia.

Entitlement to an earlier effective date for the 100 percent evaluation assigned for paranoid schizophrenia has been denied..

An evaluation of 100 percent is assigned from November 21, 1997 the date the claim for reopened benefits was received. An evaluation of 100 percent is assigned whenever there is evidence of total occupational and social impairment, due to such symptoms as: gross impairment in thought processes or communication; persistent delusions or hallucinations; grossly inappropriate behavior; persistent danger of hurting self or others; intermittent inability to perform activities of daily living (including maintenance of minimal personal hygiene); disorientation to time or place; memory loss for names of close relatives, own occupation, or own name.

REFERENCES:

Title 38 of the Code of Federal Regulations, Pensions, Bonuses and Veterans' Relief contains the regulations of the Department of Veterans Affairs which govern entitlement to all veteran benefits. For additional information regarding applicable laws and regulations, please consult your local library, or visit us at our web site, www.va.gov.

A GOOD BOOK

After careful and compassionate consideration, a decision has been reached on your claim. If we weren't able to grant some or all of the VA benefits you asked for, this form will explain what you can do if you disagree with our decision. If you don't agree with our decision, you may:

- appeal to the Board of Veterans' Appeals (the Board) by telling us you disagree with our decision
- give us evidence we don't already have that may lead us to change our decision

This form will tell you how to appeal to the Board and how to send us more evidence. You can do either one or both of these things.

WHAT IS AN APPEAL TO THE BOARD OF VETERANS' APPEALS?

An appeal is your formal request that the Board review the evidence in your VA file and review the law that applies to your appeal. The Board can either agree with our decision or change it. The Board can also send your file back to us for more processing before the Board makes its decision.

HOW CAN I APPEAL THE DECISION?

How do I start my appeal? To begin your appeal, write us a letter telling us you disagree with our decision. This letter is called your "Notice of Disagreement." If we denied more than one claim for a benefit (for example, if you claimed compensation for three disabilities and we denied two of them), please tell us in your letter which claims you are appealing. Send your Notice of Disagreement to the address at the top of our letter.

What happens after VA receives my Notice of Disagreement? We will either grant your claim or send you a Statement of the Case. A Statement of the Case describes the facts, laws, regulations, and reasons that we used to make our decision. We'll also send you a VA Form 9, "Appeal to Board of Veterans' Appeals," with the Statement of the Case. You must complete this VA Form 9 and return it to us if you want to continue your appeal.

How long do I have to start my appeal? You have one year to appeal our decision. *Your* letter saying that you disagree with our decision must be postmarked (or received by us) within one year from the date of *our* letter denying you the benefit. In most cases, you can't appeal a decision after this one-year period has ended.

What happens if I don't start my appeal on time? If you don't start your appeal on time, our decision will become final. Once our decision is final, you can't get the VA benefit we denied unless you either:

- show that we were clearly wrong to deny the benefit **or**
- send us new evidence that relates to the reason we denied your claim

Can I get a hearing with the Board? Yes. If you decide to appeal, the Board will give you a hearing if you want one. The VA Form 9 we'll send you with the Statement of the Case has complete information about the kinds of hearings the Board offers and convenient check boxes for requesting a Board hearing. The Board doesn't require you to have a hearing. It's your choice.

Where can I find out more about appealing to the Board?

- You can find a pamphlet called "Understanding the Appeal Process," and a "plain language" booklet called "How Do I Appeal," on the Internet at: **http://www.va.gov/vbs/bva/pamphlet.htm**. Both the pamphlet and booklet also may be requested by writing to Hearings and Transcription Unit (014HRG), Board of Veterans' Appeals, 810 Vermont Avenue, NW, Washington, DC 20420.

- You can find the formal rules for appealing to the Board in the Board's Rules of Practice at title 38, Code of Federal Regulations, Part 20. You can find the complete Code of Federal Regulations on the Internet at: **http://www.access.gpo.gov/nara/cfr.** A printed copy of the Code of Federal Regulations may be available at your local law library.

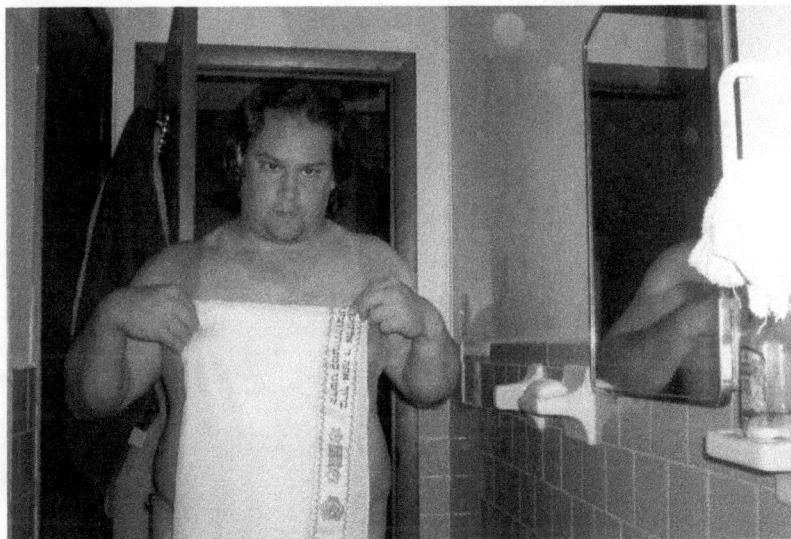

A GOOD BOOK

NATIONAL NAVAL MEDICAL CENTER
DEPARTMENT OF PSYCHIATRY
INPATIENT DIVISION
BETHESDA, MARYLAND 20889-5600

MEDICAL BOARD ADDENDUM

PATIENT NAME: LEE, SHANE E.
SSN: ███-██-████
HOSPITAL J#: 0238861
DATE OF ADMISSION: 04AUG94
DATE OF DISCHARGE:16AUG94
DATE OF BIRTH: 03NOV69

IDENTIFYING DATA: The patient was a 24 year old white male active
duty Navy E-2 with 4 years continuous service, assigned to Naval
Hospital, Portsmouth pending a Physical Evaluation Board for
Paranoid Schizophrenia and was admitted to 7 West inpatient
psychiatry at the National Naval Medical Center on 04 August 1994.

HISTORY OF PRESENT ILLNESS: The following information was obtained
from the patient and available medical records and was considered
reliable. In 1993 the patient developed delusions of being one of
the two prophets of the end times in the book of the Revelation and
was looking for "a second witness" whom he interpreted to be a
woman whom he had just met. The patient had written over 100
letters to her within a three month period and became obsessed with
fears of her being raped and also that he would be himself raped by
a thousand women. The woman had a sexual relationship with the
patient, but the patient's behavior led her to contact her command.
The patient was eventually evaluated in October of 1993 and was
found to be fit for duty and was returned to his ship. Soon
afterward, the patient began to feel that a Lieutnant on his ship
was now "a false prophet" who was trying to separate him from the
woman he was obsessed with.   The patient discontinued his
relationship with the woman but became physically involved with
three other women. Because of these relationships and his
religious convictions he felt he was no longer suited for naval
service and sought help at Naval Hospital Portsmouth. The patient
was admitted to Naval Hospital, Portsmouth (from 27 October 1993 to
10 November 1993) after having auditory hallucinations consisting
of a voice saying "Jerusalem, Jerusalem, Jerusalem" while in an
engineering space on his ship. During this hospitalization he was
given a diagnosis of Schizophrenia, Paranoid Type and was started
on Haldol 5mg po bid. He noticed no effect from medication and
discontinued it himself after his discharge from the hospital. The
Medical Board granted him 0 percent disability based on their
finding of existence prior to entry status of the diagnosis.

MEDICAL BOARD ADDENDUM ICO FA SHANE E. LEE, USN/~~ ~~ ~~

During his stay in the Medical Holding Company, he lost interest in the woman he was pursuing and became "confused" about the events that had happened previously. He no longer heard the voices. On 04 August 1994 he was sent to the National Naval Medical Center for his full and fair hearing during which he became very anxious and overwhelmed. He was unable to "understand" what was said and began "speaking in tongues" to his lawyer who recommended that he be sent to the emergency room for inpatient admission to the psychiatry ward. The patient denied suicidal or homicidal ideation and denied alcohol or drug abuse.

PAST PSYCHIATRIC HISTORY: As per HPI. No previous psychiatric evaluations.

FAMILY PSYCHIATRIC HISTORY: The patient denied any family history of suicide or mental health visits. (However see social history below.)

PAST MEDICAL HISTORY: History of closed head injury secondary to motor vehicle accident in 1988 resulting in a two day loss of consciousness with subsequent normal CT and EEG evaluations prior to entry the Navy.

ADMISSION MEDICATIONS: None. No known drug allergies.

SOCIAL HISTORY: (See Medical Board dated 01 December 1993. Additional information is as follows.) The mother had a history of drug use but encouraged the patient's religious interests which began at the age of 12 after his father was shot and killed. Per her observations, the patient was sincere but not overly zealous until he joined a specific church some time after starting boot camp in August of 1990. She stated that he became increasingly isolative and "hyperreligious" over a period of months after that time.

MENTAL STATUS EXAMINATION: Revealed moderately well groomed slightly obese white male who was alert and oriented to time, place, person and situation, casually dressed in hospital gown and pajamas, good eye contact and a slight right eye emmetropia. Speech was not pressured but normal rate, rhythm and inflection. His stated mood was "okay", and his affect was broad and congruent with mood but with slight, inappropriate mirth but otherwise relaxed. Thought process was minimally tangential but easily redirectible with no clanging or flight of ideas. His thought content on admission revolved around the events surrounding his being admitted and the impact that his "uncontrolled speaking in tongues" would have on his Medical Board. Memory was 3/3 objects at five minutes, cognition and concentration were intact to serial 7s and spelling "world" backwards. Insight was poor but judgement and impulse control were intact for medicolegal purposes.

MEDICAL BOARD ADDENDUM ICO FA SHANE E. LEE, USN/███-██-████

PHYSICAL EXAMINATION AND LABORATORY DATA: Physical exam including
neurologic examination as well as laboratory analysis to include
CBC, electrolytes, liver function studies, thyroid function
studies, RPR, urinalysis, urine drug screen and blood alcohol level
were all within normal limits or clinically unremarkable.

HOSPITAL COURSE: The patient was admitted to the inpatient
psychiatric unit on ward status.   He remained pleasant and
cooperative, participating well in individual, group, and milieu
psychotherapy.   The patient denied hallucinations and had no
episodes of uncontrolled glossolalia but has maintained a zealous
religious preoccupation with delusional content. He showed the
beginnings of insight and has in his words "begun to sort out
reality from religion", trying to discern legitimate religious
experience from uncontrolled states. He consistently denied
suicide or homicide ideation and has accumulated letters of
recommendation as material to rebut his physical evaluation board.
Projective testing reviewed by Dr. Podd, Clinical Psychologist, was
suggestive of "an affective psychosis but ... more consistent with
a diagnosis of bipolar disorder than schizophrenia..." On interview
with family members there was no evidence of psychotic or
delusional material existing prior to entry into the military.

DIAGNOSES:
AXIS I: Delusional Disorder, Grandiose Type (DSM-IV #297.1),
              DNEPTE, -- as manifested by grandiose delusions with
              a religious content stating that he is one of the two
              prophets of the end times as found in the book of the
              Revelation (this delusion has remained stable over a
              period of years.) Auditory Hallucinations on at
              least two different occasions that have not markedly
              impaired psychosocial functioning.

AXIS II: None.

AXIS III: History of closed head injury from a motor
              vehicle accident in 1988 with subsequent negative
              head CT and EEG examinations done for sleep study
              in 1990.

SHANE EDWARD LEE

NATIONAL NAVAL MEDICAL CENTER
DEPARTMENT OF PSYCHIATRY
INPATIENT DIVISION
BETHESDA, MARYLAND 20889-5600

MEDICAL BOARD ADDENDUM

PATIENT NAME: LEE, SHANE E.
SSN:
HOSPITAL J#: 0238861
DATE OF ADMISSION: 04AUG94
DATE OF DISCHARGE:16AUG94
DATE OF BIRTH: 03NOV69

IDENTIFYING DATA: The patient was a 24 year old white male active
duty Navy E-2 with 4 years continuous service, assigned to Naval
Hospital, Portsmouth pending a Physical Evaluation Board for
Paranoid Schizophrenia and was admitted to 7 West inpatient
psychiatry at the National Naval Medical Center on 04 August 1994.

HISTORY OF PRESENT ILLNESS: The following information was obtained
from the patient and available medical records and was considered
reliable. In 1993 the patient developed delusions of being one of
the two prophets of the end times in the book of the Revelation and
was looking for "a second witness" whom he interpreted to be a
woman whom he had just met. The patient had written over 100
letters to her within a three month period and became obsessed with
fears of her being raped and also that he would be himself raped by
a thousand women. The woman had a sexual relationship with the
patient, but the patient's behavior led her to contact her command.
The patient was eventually evaluated in October of 1993 and was
found to be fit for duty and was returned to his ship. Soon
afterward, the patient began to feel that a Lieutnant on his ship
was now "a false prophet" who was trying to separate him from the
woman he was obsessed with. The patient discontinued his
relationship with the woman but became physically involved with
three other women. Because of these relationships and his
religious convictions he felt he was no longer suited for naval
service and sought help at Naval Hospital Portsmouth. The patient
was admitted to Naval Hospital, Portsmouth (from 27 October 1993 to
10 November 1993) after having auditory hallucinations consisting
of a voice saying "Jerusalem, Jerusalem, Jerusalem" while in an
engineering space on his ship. During this hospitalization he was
given a diagnosis of Schizophrenia, Paranoid Type and was started
on Haldol 5mg po bid. He noticed no effect from medication and
discontinued it himself after his discharge from the hospital. The
Medical Board granted him 0 percent disability based on their
finding of existence prior to entry status of the diagnosis.

PSYCHIATRIC DISCHARGE CARE AND SUMMARY
NAVMEDCEN PTSVA 6550/77 (Rev. 5/93)

MUST BE COMPLETED BY A NURSE COPRS OFFICER

1. DISCHARGE TO: Medical Hold - Nav Med Cent Portsmouth

2. DOES PATIENT HAVE HEALTH RECORD? YES (NO) IF NOT WHERE IS IT? AT COMMAND

3. VITAL SIGNS: ARE VITAL SIGNS WITHIN NORMAL RANGE? (YES) NO (USE SAM PAN)
   T: 97° P: 58 R: 20 B/p: 136/78

4. SOMATIC COMPLAINTS: No

5. MEDICAL OFFICER NOTIFIED OF SOMATIC COMPLAINTS? YES NO N/A

6. DISCHARGE DIAGNOSIS: AXIS I: Shizophrenia, Paranoid type
   AXIS II: NONE
   AXIS III: NONE

7. MEDICATIONS: Ø
   Recommended but refused

8. PATIENT DEMONSTRATES A WORKING KNOWLEDGE OF HIS MEDICATION THERAPY. (I.E. VERBALIZES UNDERSTANDING OF TYPE OF MEDICATION, ROUTE, DOSAGE TIMES, ADVERSE REACTIONS AND SIDE EFFECTS. YES NO (IF NO EXPLAIN) N/A

9. PATIENT VERBALIZES AN UNDERSTANDING OF ACTION TO TAKE IF ADVERSE REACTIONS, SIDE EFFECTS OCCUR. YES NO (IF NO EXPLAIN) N/A

10. PATIENT (DID)/DID NOT RESOLVE ADMITTING SYMPTOMS OF: (BE SPECIFIC)
    I see that nothing can stop Jesus's will if he meant for me + Sheena to be together, we would be together. IF He meant for me to be in the Navy I wouldn't be getting discharge. So I am looking at the reality. I am not suicidal or homicidal.

11. TREATMENT CONSISTED OF: CHEMOTHERAPY____ MILIEU THERAPY ✓ GROUP THERAPY ✓ RECREATION THERAPY ✓ INDIVIDUAL THERAPY ✓ ART THERAPY ✓ OCCUPATIONAL THERAPY ✓ OTHER____ (EXPLAIN)

12. RETURN TO CLINIC/DOCTORS OFFICE/WARD ON 1130 Tues 16Nov '93 FOR with Dr. Azuar
    3rd floor Bldg 1

13. IF YOU HAVE ANY QUESTIONS CALL LT Daks 398-5350

14. SPECIAL INSTRUCTIONS: Return to limited Duty, pending EPTE Board
    Patient psychiatrically fit for same.
    EPTE - Existed prior to enlistment

15. COMMENTS: (MUST INCLUDE A STATEMENT CONCERNING THE PATIENT'S KNOWLEDGE OF AND ACCEPTANCE OF HIS ILLNESS PLUS HIS WILLINGNESS/UNWILLINGNESS TO CONTINUE/RESUME THERAPY AS NEEDED). I am not chizophrenic. I dont need medication I will see the doctors if needed.

16. ~~I HAVE RECEIVED THE MEDICATIONS LISTED ABOVE AND UNDERSTAND HOW THEY ARE TO BE USED. I FEEL COMPETENT AND AGREE TO CONTINUE WITH THE MEDICATION THERAPY ORDERED BY MY PHYSICIAN.~~ I UNDERSTAND AND AGREE TO COMPLY WITH THE INSTRUCTIONS NOTED ABOVE. I HAVE RECEIVED/(ARRANGED) TO RECEIVE MY VALUABLES.

_____   27OCT93
PATIENT SIGNATURE   SIGNIFICANT OTHER SIGNATURE

10 Nov 93   USN AD   03NOV69 ABA   _____ ENS/N
DATE OF DISCHARGE   NJO783 NAV MED CEN PORTS DISCHARGING NURSE'S SIGNATURE
                     PERSONAL DATA/PRIV ACT 1974

NAVAL MEDICAL CENTER
PORTSMOUTH, VIRGINIA 23708-5100
REPORT OF MEDICAL BOARD
EPTE, DISCHARGE - INPATIENT

NAME: LEE, SHANE E. RANK/RATE/SERVICE: EMFA/USN7AD
SSN: 20/██-██-███ REGISTER NO. 0377823
WARD: 3G, PSY. ADMISSION DATE: 27 OCT 93
TYPIST: CC DISCHARGE DATE: 10 NOV 93
DOC. NO. 6-6106 COMMAND: USS SAIPAN

D: 1 DEC 93   T: 1 DEC 93 R:

1. INTRODUCTION: This 23 year old single male, EMFA/USN7AD, with about four years active military service was admitted to the Naval Medical Center, Portsmouth, Virginia on 27 October 1993, with the diagnosis of Schizophrenia, Paranoid Type.

2. HISTORY OF PRESENT ILLNESS: The history of present illness as obtained from the patient and available records was considered reliable. The patient was self-referred to the Lafayette River Branch Mental Health Clinic (LRBMHC) where he had been previously evaluated after writing over one hundred letters to a female shipmate within a period of thirty days. He reported that on the night before admission he was told by God to go to a local convenience store where he would meet his future wife. He remained at the store from early evening until the early morning hours on the day of admission, and then slept in a nearby barn. That morning he walked to the Psychiatry Clinic where he hoped to ascertain the validity of this message from God, instead he was admitted for further psychiatric evaluation, treatment and disposition. He reported that at 12 years of age, he had been "appointed" a prophet (through the Bible), with the mission of revealing to the world that men and women are created equal. Since that time, he allegedly experienced three voices, perceived as coming from within his head. He identified these as the voices of God, Satan, and another unidentified entity. He perceived them as different in quality, but denied running commentary or derogatory comments. He denied that they were distinct personalities and claimed the voices did not take full control of his behavior.
About three months prior to admission, he met a female service member (from another ship) at a beach while overseas. They dated because he kept sending her letters almost every day informing her that she was the chosen woman for him (as he was told through the Bible). He had written her over 100 letters entreating her to join with him in his mission. He tried to minister to her through the letters, but in the long-run she reported him to her command, who informed his own command. He came to believe that a lieutenant on his ship was a "false prophet" who had schemed to come between the patient and this woman. This led to the referral on 04 Oct 93, but

LEE, SHANE E. ██-██-███ DOC. 6-6106 DATE: 1 DEC 93

A GOOD BOOK

2

he was returned to full duty. This time he met three women and,
although, he knew one woman was still married, he claimed it was
alright to have sexual relations with her because she took off her
ring. The patient decided to seek help because he felt that he was
unsuitable for Navy life, and wished to be discharged from the
service in order to pursue his holy mission. His ship was
scheduled to deploy on the day of admission and he was in an
unauthorized absence status.

3.   PAST HISTORY: The past history as obtained from the patient
and available medical records was considered reliable. The patient
was born the first of four children to a middle class family from
Garden City, Georgia which was disrupted by divorce at the
patient's age of six years. The patient had a good relationship
with his father until he was killed by gunfire when the patient was
eleven years old. He had a good relationship with his mother.
However, her parenting skills may have been diminished by drug use.
The patient was however quite defensive of his mother. He also had
a significant relationship with his maternal grandmother, who lived
nearby. His relationship with her was characterized by frequent
comments that the patient was "worthless" or "no good". Discipline
consisted of verbal rebukes and spankings. He had few friends in
childhood but many in adulthood. He dropped out of high school
during his senior year with below average grades. He had repeated
sixth and eleventh grades due to excessive absences. He later
received a Graduation Equivalence Diploma, (GED). He got along
fairly well with his teachers and peers. He stated that his
favorite subject or activity was studying the Bible. He was never
suspended. He was arrested once while in the company of a
stepbrother who had committed an unspecified crime. He endorsed
neuropathic traits of childhood, including animal cruelty and
stealing. He held several fast food jobs prior to enlistment.
The patient was involved in a motor vehicle accident with a two day
loss of consciousness at the age of 17. Medical workup proved
negative for permanent injury, and there were no sequelae. He
denied any history of physical or sexual abuse. He enlisted
because he believed it to be activity sanctioned by God. He went
to Captain's Mast one time for sleeping on watch. His evaluations
averaged 2.8 and he characterized his military performance as
"awful". His attitude had deteriorated since enlistment and he
disliked his current duties.

He described his alcohol use as rare, and denied any history
of blackouts, withdrawal phenomena or illicit drug use. He
described his personality as "open and honest". There was no other
past personal or family history of psychiatric illness, suicidal
behavior or substance abuse or dependence, except as described
above. He reported a negative sleep study by the Neurology
Department at NMC, Portsmouth while in basic training, prompted by

LEE, SHANE E.   [redacted]   DOC. 6-6106   DATE: 1 DEC 93

135

3

excessive daytime sleepiness. He denied any history of symptoms consistent with dissociative, anxiety, organic or affective disorders.

4. MENTAL STATUS EXAMINATION: Mental status examination revealed a well developed, well nourished male in no obvious distress. The patient was well-groomed and dressed appropriately in hospital pajamas. There was no psychomotor disturbance or agitation. The patient established eye contact readily. His mood was neutral to mildly anxious with affect which was inappropriately happy in view of his situation, and punctuated occasionally by inappropriate laughter. His speech was of normal rate and volume and was without pressure. There was ambivalence, tangentiality, circumstantiality, hyper-religiosity, grandiosity and paranoid ideations. He denied thought insertion or thought broadcasting. He endorsed auditory hallucinations on a daily basis, some of these being command hallucinations (voices that tell him to seek Sheena, the woman destined to be with him, and that he should spread the word of God). The patient denied suicidal or homicidal ideation. Cognition and memory were intact. Capacity for abstractions was impaired. Insight was nil and judgment was intact.

5. PHYSICAL EXAMINATION: On admission to this Naval Medical Center, the physical examination and neurological examination revealed no significant abnormalities. Routine diagnostic studies were within normal limits.

6. HOSPITAL COURSE: While hospitalized, the patient was treated with individual, group and milieu therapy. He participated well in these modalities. After an adequate period of observation, he was started on Haldol 5 mg po BID, and Cogentin 1 mg po BID. He was initially reluctant to begin medication, but agreed in order to "prove it is not needed". He announced, however, from the beginning that he had no intention of continuing medication once discharged from the hospital. There was a resolution of the circumstantiality, but otherwise little effect from the Haldol, and he continued to express his delusion, which was viewed as fixed. The patient ate and slept well and presented no management problems while hospitalized. He consistently and convincingly denied suicidal and homicidal ideations throughout his hospitalization. Serial mental status examinations revealed no evidence of organicity, major mood or anxiety disorders. He advanced to an increased privilege level. He gained no insight into his condition, but made plans for his life which were positive, if somewhat unrealistic. He was considered competent to participate in his discharge planning and did so actively. At the time of discharge, the patient was not suicidal, homicidal or committable and had received maximum benefit from inpatient hospitalization.

LEE, SHANE E. ▰▰▰   DOC. 6-6106   DATE: 1 DEC 93

A GOOD BOOK

DEPARTMENT OF VETERANS AFFAIRS
Atlanta Regional Office
PO Box 100021
Decatur GA 30031-7021

APR 1 5 2005

SHANE E LEE
185 A SMITH AVE
GARDEN CITY GA 31408

In Reply Refer To: 316/21PD/ABH
CSS 257 23 2433
LEE, S E

Dear Mr. Lee:

We made a decision on your claim for service connected compensation received on
March 25, 2004.

This letter tells you what we decided. It includes a copy of our rating decision that gives the
evidence used and reasons for our decision. We have also included information about what to do
if you disagree with our decision, and who to contact if you have questions or need assistance.

What Did We Decide?

We determined that the following conditions were not related to your military service, so
service connection couldn't be granted:

Medical Description
right eye vision loss
low back condition
coccyx injury
post traumatic stress disorder (PTSD)

**Entitlement to an earlier effective date for the 100 percent evaluation of paranoid
schizophrenia is denied.**

Your compensation payment will continue unchanged.

We have enclosed a copy of your Rating Decision for your review. It provides a detailed
explanation of our decision, the evidence considered and the reasons for our decision. You
can find the decision discussed in the section titled *"Decision."* The evidence we considered
is discussed in the section titled *"Evidence."* The reasons for our decision can be found in the
portion of the rating titled *"Reasons for Decision"* or *"Reasons and Bases."*

137

SHANE EDWARD LEE

2

CSS 257 23 2433
Lee, S E

What You Should Do If You Disagree With Our Decision.

If you do not agree with our decision, you should write and tell us why. You have *one year from the date of this letter to appeal the decision.* The enclosed *VA Form 4107, "Your Rights to Appeal Our Decision,"* explains your right to appeal.

Do You Have Questions Or Need Assistance?

If you have any questions or need assistance with this claim, please call us at 1-800-827-1000. If you use a Telecommunications Device for the Deaf (TDD), the number is 1-800-829-4833.

If you call, please refer to your VA file number 257 23 2433. If you write to us, put your full name and VA file number on the letter. Please send all correspondence to the address at the top of this letter. You can visit our web site at www.va.gov for more information about veterans' benefits.

We sent a copy of this letter to Georgia Department of Veteran Service because you appointed them as your representative. If you have questions or need assistance, you can also contact them.

Sincerely,

Kathleen R Sullivan

KATHLEEN R. SULLIVAN
Veterans Service Center Manager

Email us at: https//iris.va.gov

Enclosure(s): Rating Decision 04/11/05
              VA Form 4107

cc: SDVS

I woke up in the hospital and I thought (in amongst the enormous pain) that I had broken my back. I panicked. I thought my life was over – I thought I was paralyzed, and I didn't know why Jesus had done this to me. They told me that I was wrong, though, and that I'd broken my pelvis. So *that's* what all the pain was from.

I ruined the left side of my body entirely. I landed square on my left side, which means that it was totally wrecked. I sprained my left ankle. My left leg jammed up into my pelvis upon impact. It shattered. I then fell backwards in a heap and landed on my sacrum, which is part of the spine. I was knocked out cold from the impact.

The hospital neglected to tell me about the sacrum – they lied to me and said that I hadn't broken it. They were wrong.

They put my pelvis in an Ex-Fix. These things are designed to hold your body in place while nature heals it. I was the literal embodiment of Humpty Dumpty, and the hospital staff were straining to put me back together again. Normally an Ex-Fix is a cast for one side of the body. That wasn't deemed sturdy enough for me. They put me in a metal Ex-Fix which was drilled deep into both sides of my pelvis. I was semi-bionic now. There was a pin around my knee, holding me in place. The contraption went all the way down to the ankle, which itself was in a plaster cast.

I was black and blue. My testicles were swollen and discolored. Everything ached; everything stabbed; frankly, everything hurt.

Looking over the medical records can only truly make me understand how horrific the injuries were. The entire left side of my pelvis was pushed up nearly a whole centimeter beyond what it should've been. That movement pushed my pelvis up into my sacrum, tearing muscle from bone and ripping right through inner flesh.

I shouldn't have survived. I definitely wouldn't be able to walk.

I proved them wrong.

I was in a wheelchair after 35 days, dragging my prone body with my arms from the bed. I recovered gradually. I was up and walking with a stroller 39 days after the fall. Sure, I still was attached – hard-wired into – the Ex-Fix on my pelvis, which was using the weight of a 20lb dead weight to try and realign my pelvis in the right place, but I was walking nonetheless. I left the hospital a week later, on November 1st, and was put by the navy on convalescence leave. I was in hospital for a long time, and while there I pretty much just lay around when not doing exercises watching TV. I started watching the Power Rangers. I know that technically, it's a kids show, but I thought it was really good and most importantly, it was about karate. It was rekindling my spirit, and allowing me to vicariously act out something which I wasn't able to do while I was bedridden. My favorite was Thuy, the yellow Power Ranger. After that, my next favorite was Kim, the pink one. I thought Kim was cute, and fine as well, because she could do really good gymnastics. I found both the girls attractive, and their martial arts helped remind me of happier, healthier times. I walked out that hospital on crutches. By December 16 in Norfolk I was using a cane to get around. By New Years I was walking around without any support, all because of my faith in God and Jesus.

I was miraculously healed. I should've had serious nerve damage from the fall; I should've had serious nerve damage from the car crash before, really, but I didn't. I was healed. The doctors were speechless, totally speechless. They couldn't believe that I could walk after such a thing, but it was the Holy Ghost, by my faith in Jesus, who helped me to better understand God, who helped me to survive these three near death experiences.

That's not to say that I didn't suffer. I still feel a lot of pain today. I felt a hell of a lot of pain back then. When they removed the external fixation device, the Ex-Fix, it hardly hurt at all. That wasn't the case with the short cast from my ankle. When they took that off, all I could say over and over again was "Jesus, it hurts! Jesus! Help me!"

I have a bad taste in my mouth from the doctors who treated me. They did a good job in trying to make me right again, but they confused me with their terms. Do you think that I understood everything they told me? They told me about the injuries – about the pelvis sheer, for example – but I didn't know the exact area that it occurred. I could've sheered it below the sacrum, for all I know.

I spent most of my time convalescing trying to figure out exactly what was wrong with me, medically. I didn't understand specifically what was wrong. I had no medical training beyond CPR and my own intuition, which was fostered through watching Saturday morning cartoons. That was it. The extent of my knowledge. To say that it didn't stretch far beyond "the knee bone's connected to the thigh bone" would be about right. I didn't even properly understand the scales involved. Initially I thought that a centimeter was a millimeter (which was bad enough).

I fell on September 15. I didn't sign up to the navy medical board until November 3rd, 1994 – my 25th birthday. Some birthday it was. I signed the report the medical board in Portsmouth, VA produced. The board report said that "the member's medical condition interferes with the reasonable performance of assigned duties. On that basis, this case is referred to the Physical Evaluation Board for fitness for duty determination."

I signed the report in my tight script right under a line which read, in typewriter capitals, "I HAVE READ THE

CONTENTS OF THE ADDENDUM AND I DO NOT DESIRE TO SUBMIT A STATEMENT IN REBUTTAL." I wish I hadn't now. I was a little drugged up on all the painkillers and the treatments they had given my after the accident, and I didn't properly know what I was doing. They acted like I had purposefully refused to reopen my case. That's not the case at all. The truth is that the true seriousness of my injury was never properly explained to me. All I'm requesting now from the medical board and from the Veterans Association (all these years later, I'm still fighting them) is at least 100% back pay to when I was discharged, and on a more general crusading point that all Veterans with low disability ratings like 10 and 20% (which I fell into) be given up to two years to reopen their cases with the VA.

A year is simply not long enough! In many cases, people don't understand the full extent of their injuries, and the trauma you feel after such a monumental event like a serious injury often clouds your judgment and confuses things. For example, I got confused between the amount of time I had to reopen my case and the amount of time in the inactive reserve. It's bound to happen when you've suffered a serious life-changing event. It's especially likely when you're a paranoid schizophrenic like me.

I wasn't lazy with my rehabilitation. I worked on my pelvis injury for nearly two full years constantly doing exercise to try and bring it back to some sense of normality and strength. I have high blood pressure, and I weigh more than 225lbs. I could still maybe do some part time work (possibly under 25 hours) but I would sooner exercise and live, rather than work and maybe die.

The problem is that 25 hours isn't enough to make a living on. I'm stuck in this cycle: I'm healthy enough (in the eyes of the VA) that I don't get the right amount of disability allowance that I believe I'm entitled to, but I'm not healthy enough to make a livable wage through work. I have to muddle through and try to do the best I can. It's hard.

I kept getting stronger and stronger, though, fighting harder and harder, and I even prayed in tongues over my ankle when I was first discharged from the hospital.

I look back at the fall – the little bits of it that I can remember – and I wonder whether everything would've turned out okay had I not slipped and landed hard on the ground. I wonder what would've happened had someone not stolen my key (I believe that someone did steal my key – I think they were playing a cruel game which ended up going horrifically wrong, and they were too chicken to own up after I fell for fear of a reprimand).

For a little while after the accident and when I was slightly better I was put on light work duty. I was given the job of bringing all the medical board's reports to different doctors for them to sign. I did the job really well: so well that even though I was dropped in rank while in the navy for sleeping on watch, they bumped me back to an E-3 while being discharged, which is almost unheard of. The light work didn't last long. They let me go.

I was discharged in August 1995. I stuck around in Virginia for a bit, but trying to get my life back together was hard and was made more difficult by extenuating circumstances. My car was in an accident; someone stole my wallet. I had to wait three or four months for the navy to reissue the small check they were giving me.

I was stuck, essentially, in a rut. I tried to work at a heating and air place in Norfolk – as well as the local 7-11 – but I was having problems with my leg and my mind, so I finally packed it all in and returned back home.

My confession

selee1shane   ⌵   Subscribe

I've made plenty of mistakes in my life. There have been times, I'll freely admit it, where I've let the bad angel on my left shoulder whisper a little too loudly into my ear so that he's drowned out the good angel guiding me down a religious route. I've managed, though, to remain a good person at heart and overcome the mistakes I've made in the past to be who I am today, and to learn the truths of God.

It might shock you to learn this, but I was a fixture on the club scene at one time. I only drank occasionally, mind, and instead mostly just drank Coke or water and danced, to try and have a good time. If you want to go to the clubs to dance a little and drink just a beer or two then that's fine, and who am I or anyone else to stop you? As long as you're older than 21, and your aims are wholesome, then I am all for that. If you go, however, just to get laid, God is against that. You can behave yourself and keep your sexual urges in check. You're only making excuses to do what you want to do. Because of my disability I can't and don't really go out to clubs anymore. There were times, though, when I hooked up with a few girls when I did go to clubs. I tried to make the sex a relationship with meaning rather than just sex, but most of the time it didn't work out.

I should make it clear that for all I went to clubs, I never did drugs. I never did anything beyond dancing and listening to the music, really. I mainly tried to meet women for a relationship or something more long-term. I always behaved myself. If I went home alone, then I went home alone. So what? I had Jesus in my heart and Jesus was with me even in the club, because Jesus was in my heart. I never actually went home alone. I went home with Jesus. I was trying to be a real Christian in a tough world of teenage sex, drinking alcohol and smoking. I never really did any of those things. I may have drunk a beer when I was underage, but I didn't like it and didn't do it again much. I didn't do it because I knew full well that alcoholism ran in my family.

When I was in the navy though I went a little wild. I hooked up with a sandy blonde once when out at a club. She picked *me* up really. She wanted me as soon as she saw me. We got chatting, and bought each other drinks, and danced together. She took me in her truck to an apartment complex; she was a medic, or a core man as they're called in the navy. We made out in the apartment complex. We went to a bench and made out some more. Then we went back to the truck, and had sex there, right in the bed of the truck. I went down on her, and entered her, all of which lasted maybe five or 10 minutes. When it was over, we exchanged numbers and ship info, but I never saw her again. I was a little nervous, because we didn't use protection. I never heard from her again, though, so I presume nothing came of it. About a year later I thought I might've run into her briefly, but she took off before I could take a proper look and see if it was her. Who knows.

My view when it comes to sex is that you can do anything, anything at all. From the Kama Sutra to tantric sex, it's all fair game, as long as you realize it isn't just about pleasure alone but is done with the aim of having and raising a family one day. If you don't want a family eventually, the only thing you can do is masturbate. It's simple. When you have sex, you are taking the first step towards marriage and spending the rest of your lives together. If you don't want to do that, don't have sex. Standing up and having sex in different positions isn't a problem for God, though for some of the more adventurous positions you need to be limber, which is another benefit that doing karate when I was younger gave me.

There was one girl called Maribel who I really took a shine to. I met Maribel during my navy days, at the Burger King near the base we were posted at. I noticed her behind the counter when she was working, and she noticed me too. I let her make the first move: I learnt that it's better for me to let the woman make the sexual advances because of my eye, than me try to have sex by making moves on women. It didn't work up until I was 21 and someone made a move on me and took my virginity, so I realized that I should let the woman do all the work. I responded to her move, and got Maribel's number. We would call each other back and forth, but hadn't been on a proper date until Valentine's Day. We had our first date then, and we went to a nearby motel and made love. We would get together as often as we could, and it was pretty great. We would have sex in the back seat of my Chevy Cavalier, and in the shower – wherever we could find time and space to do it. Eventually I got an apartment of my own in Norfolk, VA, near to Old Dominion University, which made it easier for us to meet up. She was born on the same day as my dad – July 3 – which I thought was fate and made me think I should marry her if she could deal with me being one of the two witnesses.

Maribel would call me when she finished work for the day at Burger King and I would drive around and pick her up. We'd go back to mine for a booty call. Things were going great – but then her mom found out that I had psychological problems and made it clear she didn't want her daughter seeing me anymore. We still tried to sneak around her mom's prying eyes, and did for a little while, but it got too difficult so we tailed off our relationship.

It was made easier to break up with Maribel when she moved in with another man. She swore she wasn't having sex with him, but frankly she could've been telling me one thing and doing something entirely different. I'm ashamed to admit that I got upset and angry, and wanted revenge on her (because I truly believed she was sleeping with this guy she moved in with), and so I did cheat on her.

The first girl I had sex with I met at a friend's birthday party. The girl was the birthday boy's girlfriend, but she was there as a sort of stripper. She did a little show, and all the guys got excited. I wound up hooking up with her, but she turned sour on me.

I went to some strip clubs while I was in the navy. I went to a couple in Norfolk, VA and Portsmouth, VA near the navy base, and sometimes I went to ones in Savannah, GA. If you're single, it's ok. It's fine, as long as you obey the rules (and often, the guys they have in there make sure that you obey the rules to the letter of the law). I wouldn't drink much and kept my faculties in there. I'd get a couple of lap dances, but always behave myself.

I once travelled to South Carolina for a strip club. I went across the Talmage Bridge a while back into Hinesville and went to a club there where they had Asian women. I was in a dream world.

Sometimes I just go to strip clubs to get a Coke and talk to the bartender. I don't even sexually respond to the women unless I'm getting a lap dance. I will admit (because it's important to be frank) that I will fantasize about the girl that I've got the lap dance off later in the night. I can't – nor would I – endorse strip clubs for everyone. Some people can't handle them. Some people can. If you can't handle them; if you feel uncomfortable, it's simple: don't go.

I've paid for sex once. I'm not proud of it, but I did. I went to a Taco Bell in Norfolk, VA, near the navy base, and while there I started up a conversation with a woman in line. Her name was Lisa (I should point out now that she was a completely different person to the Lisa I dated when I was 16). She started talking to me, and the conversation eventually came around to her asking for $160 for me to have sex with her. She wanted me to pay to have sex with her, but I only had $80 on me, even after the Taco Bell. I bargained with her, and gave her my license as makeweight for the money and promised to give her the rest later on, so we had sex in her car. We did it from behind: she lay over her seat in her car, and I had sex with her doggy style. I never did give her the rest of the money. I felt too guilty about paying for sex. I'm the first to say I'm not good by my righteousness, but by letting Jesus make me righteous. I'm good by following the Holy Ghost within me, and by admitting my mistakes, like I am just now. I'm learning from them. That makes a man a good man: his ability to realize his mistakes, and to learn from them.

Basically I know that I *can* behave myself, but I am often around (and particularly while I was in the navy I was around) crazy people who don't want to love deeply. They want to do what they want to do, and you get swept up along with it.

I'm going to be frank with my sexual confessions, because it's only through doing that that you can learn not to follow my lead, and to understand that fundamentally I am good because I don't shirk from admitting my mistakes.

I tried to sleep with a girl cousin of mine when I was about five or six. I took a bath with a male cousin, and we pretended that we were girls by tucking our penises between our legs. It was just pretend. Later I learned that it was wrong and unnatural to do this, so I quickly stopped. Some people say with men and with the Beast alike, with Judas and Lucifer, it's all the same. Once you sin, you can't repent or admit your mistake or stop doing it. Once a gay, always a gay. Once a cheater, always a cheater.

That's wrong.

It's a lie.

Its aim is to get you to not repent, to not accept the love of God and the mercy of confession. You can repent, you can be loved by God and you can accept mercy so long as you confess and atone for your sins.

I tried to sleep unsuccessfully with about three other girls, which I'm truly sorry for. I liked kissing girls. I had a new girlfriend every year from the age of seven to 10, and would make out with them *constantly*. At a summer camp called the Fresh Air Home, I got my first hard-on. I was 10. I was standing in line with a bunch of other boys, waiting to get washed by some older female counselors. It got me excited. I'm willing to admit it.

I was with 17 different women from August 1991 to October 1998. That's a lot of women for that space of time for a religious man. I'm not proud of it, but I was confused by the church I was with at the time, and suffered from some tremendous mental problems which clouded my judgment. If I could go back and change everything, I would. I wouldn't have been with those 17 women. I would've made better decisions. But we live by our failures and well as our successes.

Once I ran into a woman on a bus who gave me her number and address and told me to stop on by. She was being fairly clear that she wanted to have sex. When I got my car back (it had broken down which was why I was taking the bus) I went to her place, but she had another guy there. She wanted both of us to have sex with her – at the same time, but I wasn't into that. I demurred. She wound up taking me into the bathroom and performing oral sex on me, but it took so long that I'm sure her other friend thought we were having full sex in there. I lasted about five minutes. She let me do it in her mouth, but she spit it out eventually.

I didn't like that experience. It felt like she was trying to get me off quicker than I was ready to ejaculate. She really would've done us both a favor if she had had sex with me there in the bathroom. I only like straight sex with penis in the vagina, really. I've never had anal sex with someone. I'm just not that sort of person.

I would like to apologize to any woman out there – like Sheena, Daphne and Maribel – to whom I may have done wrong unintentionally. I've never harmed them physically, but I feel like I may have wronged them. I'm sorry for that.

I let the fallen gods exploit me, which was a big mistake. I wouldn't do that again – not ever. That's why I've been celibate for more than two years: because I love God.

A female responds to a man sexually by getting wet in her vagina. She lubricates herself in response to a man that she is sexually attracted to. But it's worth pointing out that the first person you respond to this way isn't necessarily the man you are supposed to marry. Most young women and mature ladies alike respond to a number of different men in an open environment, and likewise so do men in their own way. Lust and love are two different things. Love is patient. Love can wait. Sex can't. Love can masturbate to one person if they are in a serious relationship, and wait for the right time to be with the person they love, isn't afraid to marry. Sex doesn't do that.

Can a woman or a man cheat on a person they are married to? The answer is yes, of course, but that is part of the point of a woman being a virgin. A man is to test the woman's word. In the olden days, the man would bring a white towel to bed on his wedding night, and was to place it on the bed sheets. The woman was to lay on top of it, and would bleed on the towel as a token of her virginity. Back then, if the woman wasn't a virgin – if she didn't bleed – the man was free to annul the marriage and seek another woman to marry.

That doesn't happen today. Nowadays, the attitude towards sex is all wrong. Men and women alike are throwing their virginity away like it's the plague, or like they'll be a virgin sacrifice to Satan or something. This is, of course, crazy. Everything happens on the earth in its due season: you can't rush things. It all happens when it should either by nature or by man messing around with nature. No virgin sacrifice to Satan is going to change that. In God's eyes, the way a woman sacrifices her virginity is that she keeps her virginity intact until she finds the one man who truly loves her, and will marry her and treat her right. Then, and only then, does she give up her virginity. As men and women we're altogether too quick to give up too easily on that initial spark, the electrical feeling that brings two people together. Lust *can* become love, I'll grant that.

You've got to respect women. Men are far too willing to throw away their respect for women. You can't beat women. That's totally wrong. Yet even though I won't hit a woman, that doesn't mean that it can't happen if the woman says the wrong thing.

Take Myron's ex-girlfriend, for example. Her name was Allery. She was talking trash about me being a layabout, and blaming me for the problems she and Myron were having with their relationship. The three of us were out at the Burger King off Eisenhower Drive in Savannah, and Myron had gone to the bathroom. She went into the Burger King to get a straw for her drink. I was standing outside. As she came out, I put my foot in her face like Bruce Lee does (all without hitting her) like I was in Fists of Fury and told her straight. I said: "Bitch, quit talking bad about me, or I will end you."

I walked off. Myron thought I had kicked her, which is ridiculous. I wouldn't have kicked her: I was just letting her think I would at the time. If I had kicked her, I would've ended her.

I've had some problems with women. I was obsessed a little – by my own admission – with a girl called Sheena who I met in the military. I met her in May 1993, and was infatuated. I guess I have problems taking no for an answer, and I'm much more personable than other people. I think that might have freaked her out. We dated for a bit, but she wanted to break it off and I didn't. I kept acting like we were going out, and she eventually took it to the naval authorities.

They prepared a report, which I'll quote from here to prove that I'm willing to present both the positive and negative halves of me. The naval psychologist assessed me and interviewed the both of us about our experiences. His report wasn't all that flattering to me.

> The patient was referred due to his sending approximately 100 letters to a female AD/USN he had met in May '93 despite several written requests by the female for him to stop. Over time these letters became increasingly aggressive in there [sic] sexual tone and religious claims. The SM stated the belief, based on a dream he

had before enlisting, that he was to be a prophet to the world as described in the Bible. He felt this woman was to be his bride and a prophet with him.

He admitted that his faith was misplaced and he will no longer pursue her in any fashion. From communicating with the SH's H.O. and upon interviewing the patient, it is determined that his Axis I diagnosis does not interfere with his work performance, although is [sic] has been consistently poor.

I can't help it if I get obsessive. It's only because God tells me that I will find the right woman. For example, the first time I admitted myself to the Lafayette River Mental Health Center – the first time that I realized that I had some sort of mental problem – was when the night before I admitted myself I was told by God to go to a local store. I was told that if I went there (he was very clear), I would meet my future wife. Who wouldn't do that? Who wouldn't want to meet their future wife? I went to the convenience store, and I stayed there until I was going to meet my wife. I got there about 5pm, and I didn't leave until the sun rose the following morning.

I was tired by then, of course, so I found a barn nearby that had an unlocked door and slept there until I was fully rested. I was confused as to why what seemed like such a categorical statement from God hadn't come true. I presumed that I had misconstrued it in some way. So I went to the medical center, and wanted to find out whether it was God that was crazy or me. I told the psychologist – Dr. Karcher – about the moment I had when I was 12, when God came to me and told me my mission in life was to spread His word that all men and women are created equal. I just wanted to be open and honest. I felt that was important, just as I feel it's important now. You've laid out your money to read this, and I feel a duty as a human being to be as honest with you as humanly possible.

Also, while I was away with the navy my other friend David married a girl called Angel. I hadn't seen David in about a year because of one thing or another, so I popped by his house while on leave when I had my Grand Am. David and Angel had a couple of daughters, and were trying for a little boy. We were just talking normally about it, imagining what it would be like and how David and Angel would be blessed if they could have a boy to join the two daughters.

I don't know whether Angel didn't like me or something, because halfway through the conversation she said offhand something that sounded like I would have molested their son had they had one. Obviously I didn't take very kindly to this. Before I knew it I had slapped her across the face.

I was having problems at the time. The navy guys were giving me a hard time, and I had just come through all the problems surrounding Sheena, who I met on the ships. I must've misheard her, and I snapped. I hit Angel.

She got upset and angry – as did David. David got really mad, and challenged me to a fight. I really didn't want to fight my best friend, and I thought maybe I had misunderstood what Angel had said, so I apologized right away and explained that I didn't understand what she had said, and told her that in my mind it sounded like she was implying I would have molested their son had they had one. It turns out that not only was I slapping her (which was bad enough): I was also rekindling unhappy memories. She had been beaten by her father when she was younger, and me slapping her didn't help matters at all.

I managed to cool them both down and promised them it would never happen again. It didn't.

It wasn't to end happily for David and Angel, though. Later on, Angel wound up cheating on David, and they broke up and divorced. Once they had split, he came up to me and told me he was sort of glad I had slapped her, because he knew even then that she was no good in the long run.

I find the whole gender divide thing ridiculous. It gets so bad with the division between the sexes that only a woman is thought to be good at reading and comprehension skills. Baloney. The same thing with men: they're supposed to be better at math. All these skills are necessary for both genders to make it through life. Ignorance *is not* bliss. Don't let anyone tell you that it is. It will send you to the grave faster than anything else in this world will, and hell is the grave. It's death – it's separation of the spirit from the body. That's not a good fate.

You have to investigate everything, I feel, to be able to best make a decision on your belief. I looked a little into the occult to see what it was all about when I was younger. I even had a book of spells, which I got through Little Roddy. I tried a bunch of the spells in there, but none of them worked, save for one. The one that did work was a spell to get rid of a headache, which involved putting your head under cold running water and saying a chant (which was so ridiculous I can't even remember it now). That spell did work, but because the others didn't, I lost interest. I was also wary that if any of them did work that I didn't want to delve into the more macabre and grotesque spells. I didn't want to be calling up the dead or any demons or doing animal sacrifices.

Now I'll freely admit (as I've been throughout this autobiography, and throughout my life really) that I hear voices in my head a little. I have to carefully discern them. You may not hear voices: if so, good on you. I'm glad you don't, but I do. I'm putting the information out there for you, so you don't have to go through what I had to go through to learn the ways of the Bible. I had to fight demons and still have to listen to my good and bad side battling over me. I hope you don't have that.

But, if you're to walk by faith in the word of God and not by sight alone, you need to be more than just a hearer of my words. You need to be a doer too.

SHANE EDWARD LEE

People get up in arms because I have a rather unique take on religion, and spreading the word of the Bible. I'm unafraid to say that I will repeat the Bible word-for-word, and will repeat the unfashionable, or unpalatable bits just as readily as the acceptable sections.

A lot of ministers don't do that. I know that my pastor was always cherry picking the best sections of the scriptures that best portrayed his standpoint. I believe that does a disservice to the Bible. Either you believe in it all, or you don't believe at all. I'm very keen that people recognize that they have to submit themselves to the scriptures in its entirety, and follow their path, rather than simply pick and choose which bits they want to follow, or which bits they want to believe.

A lot of Biblical commentaries leave out bits that might not fit in with how they want their religion to be perceived. I'm not one for shying away from the truth, as demonstrated all the way through this autobiography. Revelations 1:13 is a pretty incredible verse of the Bible. In it, it explains how Jesus – the son of God – was actually a hermaphrodite, a concept overlooked by most Biblical scholars for one reason or another. The text reads "and in the midst of the seven candlesticks one like unto the Son of man, clothed with a garment down to the foot, and girt about the paps with a golden girdle."

Now I don't know if you know this, but "paps" is the Old English word for female breasts. I've looked it up. Jesus had female breasts. This means Jesus was a true hermaphrodite. It means he was neither male nor female, Jew nor gentile, bonded nor free. It's an important concept to understand. It depends on what version of the Bible you have as to whether it says "paps" or not. When you look at the original Greek, the word is *mastois* in the original language. It says "a proper female breast; pap". Moreover, Luke 11:27 reads "and it came to pass, as he spake these things, a certain woman of the company lifted up her voice, and said unto him, Blessed is the womb that bare thee, and the paps which thou hast sucked." You go to the Greek and the word is *mastoi* – it's the same definition. You go to Luke 23:29: "for, behold, the days are coming, in the which they shall say, Blessed are the barren, and the wombs that never bare, and the paps which never gave suck." Look at the definition of the word: it says "female breast". Jesus was somehow both genders. He had a girdle about his chest to conceal this fact. John, seeing Jesus in his glory, noticed that. That seems to indicate that Jesus is more than just a man. In Galatians 3:28, it's even clearer.

I said earlier that Jesus was neither male nor female, Jew nor gentile, bonded nor free. That's because I was quoting almost verbatim Galatians 3:28, which I believe sums up entirely that Jesus is a hermaphrodite; that he has both – or neither – gender. That passage reads "there is neither Jew nor Greek, there is neither bond nor free, there is neither male nor female: for ye are all one in Christ Jesus." What we know as male and female, is one in Jesus. We're baptised into his body, as he is taking on the whole body of Christ. Some don't understand this; they shy away from it, because as a message it's not as popular. But I'm not afraid to talk about it. I believe we need to give our whole trust over to the scriptures, and I believe we therefore need to take them at face value. We can't sanitise them to fit what we *want* our religious beliefs to be. That's not how religion works. The Bible was written for a reason. You can't twist it to mean whatever you want. That's wrong.

If you're interested in thinking about these things for yourself, then great. I like to guide people, but I don't want to proscriptively lead them by the hand through the scriptures. I believe that it's important to take people part of the way, and to guide them in the right direction, but I wouldn't want to take away the joy of finding out more about your religious beliefs from people. That's partly why my religious zeal is so strong: I found things out through my own initiative, and it made my faith that much stronger. One brilliant reference work is Strong's Exhaustive Concordance of the Bible. It takes the whole Bible – the entire thing – and indexes it. It doesn't try to provide Biblical commentary: it allows you to make up your own mind and find your own discoveries. But it does link the words used in the Bible to each other across passages, and it also explains how they came to be, linking them to their Greek and Hebrew roots. The Concordance was created by Dr. James Strong and a team of more than 100 fellow researchers in 1890. It keeps getting updates, but it's fairly encyclopaedic already to be honest. It's what I used to make my discovery that Jesus was a hermaphrodite. It opens up the text exponentially.

People have attacked me for saying this. For telling the truth.

I've written about it extensively online, and I've also uploaded more than one Youtube video explaining it over the years. Each time, I've been attacked on both sides: by non-believers who think that I am ridiculous for putting such credence in the Bible (which they're entitled to say, but I feel sorry for them for not believing in Christ Almighty and for the penance they will have to pay upon death), and by religious people who would rather not that their saviour is neither a man nor a woman. It's hard to take all their barbs. But I take strength from the fact that I am uncovering the Seven Seals – the most hidden knowledge in the Bible, only uncoverable to those who have been chosen and have the power to decipher it – for the masses. Jesus was a hermaphrodite. I'm sorry to break it to people, but I will serve Him anyway. People seem troubled by me uncovering this, and they find it uncomfortable that there is a reference to his true gender confusion in the Bible. They point to the fact that he is referred to elsewhere as the Son of Man. But they overlook the point that the basis of hermaphrodism means that you can refer to Him as either gender. In fact, all that my true reading of the scriptures does is make Jesus more universal. The problem is that people are so closed-minded that they're unwilling to accept something which doesn't tally with their selective view, even if it ends up making their saviour seem all the better for it. I'm ashamed to say that I had to call one of my Youtube commenters who disagreed with me a dumbass. When you have mental problems like I do, you become very tetchy. You don't take criticism all that well, especially when it's criticism of the truth, or of a wholesome effort. I'm trying to improve people's perceptions of religion, and I'm trying to directly improve their way of life by getting them to accept God and live their lives in His manner. When people attack me for that, I get upset.

I also get upset when people attack me for changing my story.

People have accused me of creating a fiction – of lying, at worst – about certain parts of my life.

That is categorically untrue.

Everything that I've said here happened, to the best of my knowledge. The problem is that the human mind is fallible, and because mine isn't as ship-shape as other people's, I'm more prone to factual slippage.

For example, I thought that I was admitted to the hospital following my car crash ten days earlier than I actually was. In fact, I thought that I was admitted to a different hospital. But I have paranoid schizophrenia, and I had just suffered an incredible trauma directly to my head. People's memories merge all the time: who hasn't conflated two stories into one when retelling them at a twenty year delay? The problem is that my memory is more fallible than others people's. The human mind, besides, is plenty fallible. We're not designed to have perfect memories.

I've done a lot of reading around the subject, because it is something which profoundly affects me. I've been particularly interested in reading around the theories of autobiography since I decided to undertake writing this book, because I wanted to see how truthful I can be, given that I really wanted to present the most truthful version of events that I could. It's a large anchor in my life, and telling the truth as best I can is something I pride myself on.

But I've learnt through reading some highly intelligent men that you can't necessarily be one hundred percent accurate in what you're saying or writing. David Hume was an old Scottish philosopher, who wrote a book called *A Treatise of Human Nature* in 1739. Though he was writing before most of the psychologists made their name, and Jungian outlooks became the norm, he tells an incredible human truth about us all.

To him, personal identity

> is nothing but a bundle or collection of different perceptions, which succeed each other with an inconceivable rapidity, and are in a perpetual flux and movement. Our eyes cannot turn in their sockets without varying our perceptions.

That's an important point. Our outlook changes, depending on our circumstances. When I'm having a good day, when people have been nice to me on Youtube and I'm feeling fitter and healthier than normal, I'm more likely to remember my past in a more positive way. When I'm aching badly from the injuries, and the voices in my head are particularly loud, and people on Youtube are being particularly malicious, I'm more likely to look back with sorrow at my mistakes. Hume continues:

> Our thought is still more variable than our sight; and all our other senses and faculties contribute to this change; nor is there any single power of the soul, which remains unalterably the same, perhaps for one moment. The mind is a kind of theatre, where several perceptions successively make their appearance; pass, re-pass, glide away, and mingle in an infinite variety of postures and situations.

That's my theory of autobiography, informed by some thinking from a Scottish man more than 250 years ago. All I can present to you is the best truth I know. I'm never going to get the absolute truth, but I can try and get as close to it as possible. That's what I'm trying to do here. My mind may have failed me; it's bound to. But

I'm telling you the best truth that I know at this point, and I try to back my version of the truth with empirical data.

For example, my claims to be a paranoid schizophrenic are backed up by medical reports which say that. The story of how I ended up in Memorial Hospital after the car crash just before my 17th birthday is partly informed by my mom's memory of it when she told me about it later on (which itself is fallible and open to personal interpretation) and partly by the cold hard fact of pen on paper and the medical records.

In many ways, I'm trying to do something similar to a Genevan philosopher who was around at the same time as David Hume. His name was Jean-Jacques Rousseau. Eight years before he died, he attempted to atone for all the sins he had committed by writing an autobiography called *Confessions*. His task, he said, was "without precedent". "I propose to show my fellows a man as nature made him, and this man shall be myself." Like Rousseau, I believe that "I have concealed no crimes, added no virtues; and if I have sometimes introduced superfluous ornament, it was merely to occupy a void occasioned by defect of memory".

I'm trying to give you the best truth that I can, without concealing anything bad, or presenting myself as a paragon of virtue. If I make a mistake or two along the way in retelling that, it's not a conscious fault. I'm not trying to actively make myself seem better. I've freely admitted that I have faults, and that I have a good and a bad angel on each shoulder. Sometimes I listen to my bad angel too readily; sometimes I ignore the good one.

The problem is that no-one can tell a totally objective truth. There will be subjectivity in there, because I've seen what I've seen through my own eyes and no-one else's. I've tried to keep that subjectivity to a minimum, but in many ways it's unavoidable. It's important to point out though, that despite my best attempts, nothing in this book – no reminisces – can be wholly truthful. All of them will be tinged with my point of view. The best I can do is try and cancel out the personal opinions as best as I can and just give you the facts.

I tried writing a book about my life once before. I didn't get all that far. In many ways, it acted as a firs draft for this. I eventually finished the first attempt, but it wasn't very good. It was disordered and confused and all in the wrong order – a bit like my life. But I showed it to my family, and they seemed to like it. So I endeavored that I would eventually try again. What you're reading is the product of that endeavor.

People are also scared of me and my take on the Bible because I can speak in tongues. Some people find this alarming: they shouldn't. Glossolalia (or speaking in tongues) is normal, and is not sinister. It proves that I am one of the two witnesses sent by God to decipher his sayings and his secrets, and spread them to the world.

Some people think that it's a load of baloney. They believe that when I upload videos of me talking in tongues to the internet, that I'm just making it up. They have no respect for the religious aspect of the skill, and the seriousness of it all. They believe I'm just wagging my tongue in different ways, talking nonsense to anyone who will listen. They are wrong. It's a skill which I lucked upon.

I was trying to just be a normal Christian guy, living his life piously, not doing much more than the average Christian. But in July 1993, my life changed. God obviously decided that he had more in store for me. More even than I or my Christian brothers and sisters might want to admit.

I had gone to Haifa, Israel on a pilgrimage of sorts. I wanted to get closer to God, and to the places where all the events of the

Bible took place. I wanted to be holier. It was baking hot, as Israel is during that time of the year, and I truly felt like I was being deposited right in the middle of the Bible. I could imagine the Biblical figures travelling through the desert in this heat, the sun beating down on the backs of their necks, dreaming of the next drink of water from a mirage or pool somewhere.

As part of my trip in Haifa I decided to go to Mount Carmel, where Elijah lived in a little grotto. It was there that the Lord God was proven to be the true deity of Israel by Elijah's challenge to 450 prophets of another religion. It's an important place in Christianity.

I was taken up with the spirit of God while I was on Mount Carmel. I was by myself, choosing to take the pilgrimage properly and without interference from anyone else. I went up and down the mountain, singing to myself to pass the time. I wasn't singing anything in particular – just whatever syllables came to mind, trusting in my instinct. I sung and sung loudly, and I must've sounded good. No-one complained or said a single word against me, so it must've been impressive.

I had been granted the gift of tongues, and I was speaking holy words. Since then I've tried to teach others, but it's barely worked. I guess only I was meant to be given the gift of speaking in tongues. Jesus brought me up to a higher level. He did it with a point. The pastor of the church I went to in Norfolk, VA at the time was a cruel man who was trying to deny my assertions that I was one of the Biblical two witnesses. I believe that God gave me the gift of tongues to prove the pastor wrong, and to demonstrate to him and to skeptics and unbelievers that I was someone who could be trusted to spread the word of God honestly and with heart.

People today are still wary, but they don't realize that there is such a thing as tongues. Through careful honing of my ability,

SHANE EDWARD LEE

I've managed to not only speak tongues, but to transcribe it into text when needed. For example, here's a passage in tongues that I was given while writing this book:

> Alhaaayu in teiqamf leland peladn wiealnf wsgsmcaharda poesl ensdla qwpeda; qiesd ut deodld an quepedlft. Oeamdmd elmdd epald eldgledpg qpqaldnv bfndlaoe ndoral yuporn et adlvmva. Eurpael monenal potepal runyalelq qlddmd – qoedndla teoend unopeant – wle ripdd munnipolis ashjij. (Ropharis ut jumpah roiltek.)
>
> Yahmuh in juliapod tuaru bolo qua smoemfmadl ex powqlegbyru.
>
> In ereos tylipo qumbar wulu sinddmaldld, kindpad ij monbolora pipipqual.

In April 1995 I had a girlfriend from the Philippines. I thought at the time – because of coincidences – that she was my wife. She eventually filed a stalking charge on me, but it was dropped because she didn't follow through with it. I wanted to prove to her that God wanted her to be my wife, and me her husband, so I asked God for help.

I asked him in tongues for help, and he answered me. I spoke to her and sang to her in Tagalog (which is the Filipino language). That might not be that impressive – but I hadn't studied the language at all. I didn't even have sight of a phrasebook! I said something like the words "Pakasalan mo ako, hindi sha, mahal na mahal kita, miss na miss kita". When I eventually consulted the Filipino phrasebook, I learnt that what I said to her – the words breathed into me by God – was "marry me, not him. I love you. I miss you".

Using tongues is a good thing, not a bad thing. My step-brother Mark was a close friend of mine as well as pretty much family. After I'd been in the car crash the two of us got into trouble

168

with the police for burglary. We only did it once, and I was taken advantage of by my brother. He was piggybacking on my studying about the art of the ninja, which I was keen about after my karate.

In the art of the ninja there are supposedly two paths you can take in life. One, the white path, is where you study for studying's sake, and to protect against using the art of the ninja, and the other is the black path. In the black path, you actually use the knowledge and art of the ninja. I was just talking about it – how it would be cool to follow the black path, and to act like ninjas and use their stealth and training – but Mark was serious.

We were going to burglarize a house.

I couldn't believe we were actually going out there and doing this. It seemed so wrong. But by that point Mark had inculcated me to the point where it didn't seem so bad. We were both quiet when we needed to be, stealthily avoiding detection while sneaking across yards. I accidentally stepped on a twig when we were near the house, all dressed in black, and alerted the dog they had. It barked really loudly and we had to stay perfectly still until it calmed down and we could continue.

He had a plan, and he enacted it. I thought he was playing; I knew I was. But no, Mark actually went into the house we were staking out. He came back with some loot under his arm, and I was shocked. I was in way above my depth here, and I was uncomfortable.

We were caught, and he hosed me on the deal. I didn't really care about it, but he wasn't going to share the stuff he had stolen from the house. It was all irrelevant anyway. We were caught, and he told on me like it was my fault when we were caught. I learned my lesson, and did what the court told me to do (they gave me community service, which I completed just before I joined the navy). I never did it again.

Mark was a bad influence on me, truth be told. He tried to get me to smoke – but I didn't inhale. He likewise offered me a joint when I was young – but again, I didn't inhale. Mark did. I got mad at him for doing it.

Though he committed a crime and tried to wrongly implicate me in it, I forgave my step-brother. A little later on he got a brain tumor, and the doctors said it was really bad. He was committed to Memorial with serious health problems. I went to Memorial and the chapel there, and I knelt down and prayed for him. I prayed in tongues, so that God would hear me better, and know that this was important; that it was coming from one of his two chosen witnesses. Lo, he recovered! The tumor disappeared and he was better again.

I'm not saying the doctors didn't help him too. Look, we both did what we could. But my prayers, and my use of tongues, was all for the good. We got rid of that tumor, and Mark was forgiven and okay.

He later got ill again with the same thing – it came back. I was all ready to pray for him again, to dig down deep into my store of compassion and to pray to God to make him better again. But he didn't want that. He wanted to die. I felt bad, but I let him choose his path. I prayed, still, but I prayed for him to be taken by the angels into paradise, and to sleep sweetly and quietly when he got there.

Over the years I've had to do an awful lot of praying for an awful lot of people. I lost my Grandma – Meema – in 2003 to cancer. She smoked for years, and for all those years I prayed for her not to get cancer. For a while it worked, but eventually God decided it was time to take her. When she got the cancer, it hit her like a wrecking ball all at once. The years of smoking that she did all crept up on her. She had ovarian and colon cancer. We hoped still that she would heal and recover, but she didn't. I knew really that she wouldn't. It was intuition. The night before she died, I had a dream of me standing over her, praying desperately for her to recover. In the dream I was working for a labor company and was dropping someone off, going down the 5-16 between Savannah and Garden City. I was halfway down the road – about five miles in – near a place called Sam's Wholesale, when I heard an almighty scream. I knew right then that something was wrong. When I got back, the dispatcher called me into her office and I knew. I dreamt that I knew because I had heard my mom screaming when she heard about her mom dying, even though she was miles away. It wasn't with my physical ears that I heard the scream – don't get me wrong. It was with my spiritual ears. The angel of Yahweh had made me aware that something bad was about to happen. That was a sad time.

She was followed in rapid succession by my Aunt Francine and Uncle Harvey the next year. Aunt Francine had colon cancer, and Uncle Harvey had a brain tumor.

My ex-wife Daphne also has a brain tumor, but has so far survived and is still living with it today. She takes life day-by-day. I call her every so often, and send my son a card and a present for his birthday and Christmas. He gets part of my disability money as child support through Social Security Disability, just like I did when my dad died.

It isn't my choice – and it isn't my preferred choice either (I would like to be earning a good wage which I can give him part of, but not being able to work a proper job I can't) – but I do the best I can for him. I do the best I can on the faith that God has given me in Him. When I can walk I walk for as long as I can until I hurt again. I then lay down however long I have to until I can muster the strength to get up again. That's how I function now. I work out in spurts of faith, go to the mall in spurts of faith, buy groceries in spurts of faith. If I have to lay down afterwards, and if it has to be from 30 minutes to a couple of hours, then so be it. I do it regardless, even though it may hurt like hell afterwards.

I do it all because of God, and because He has chosen me to be one of his benefactors, and someone who resultantly spreads His word on earth. It – and my general appearance – has gotten me into trouble in the past. While I was working at the Roger Wood Packing Company after school and before I joined the navy, I was jumped by five African-American teenagers. I don't know why. I was on my way to the movies on the bus (something I usually did most weeks without trouble) and this one time I got jumped.

I was sitting by an African-American girl, and I don't think she realized that I have my astigmatism. She must have noticed my bad eye, and took it the wrong way like I was winking at her (people often do this. I suppose it's a common misunderstanding, and they can't be blamed for their ignorance of eye trouble). One of her friends – I presume: he could just have been another African-American who had no connection to the girl I was sitting next to – started fronting up and acting like he wanted to start something with me. I'm religious, and I'm docile, and I didn't want to start anything, but by the same token I'm not one to step down and let people walk all over me. So I stood up to him. I'm not ashamed to admit it. I stood up to him, but hadn't realized he was in a group of friends. Next thing I know there were four other guys surrounding me on the bus and I was trapped! I had nowhere else to go, and they started pounding on me. The fight was broken up by another African-American man – an older one – but I had to suffer the indignity of sitting on the same bus as my attackers for the rest of the ride. I didn't let them know that they got to me, just like I try not to let the trolls on the internet that attack me know that they've hit a nerve.

Despite being picked on, and despite the tremendous pain which I felt as the result of my car accident, I still tried to keep in shape. Perhaps, deep down, it was precisely *because* I was getting picked on that I tried to bulk up. I guess I reasoned that if I was more able to look after myself, and appeared stockier, people might be less likely to try and pick a fight with me. I was in excellent shape physically back then before the navy – the peak of my fitness, really. I would run and walk through the trailer park where I lived at the time, and would ride my bike regularly. I once rode my bike marathon distance – 26 miles – from Springfield to Garden City, GA. That was a *long* ride; it took me a few hours. But it was worth it. I hurt after, but I felt great.

I look back on those days and wish that I could still do the same. My body's been broken down too long to recover and ride 26 miles again. I don't have the impetus anymore. Where there once was muscle, there's now flab. I still do work out, but I can't do as much as I once did – and besides, when I do, it doesn't make a difference to the shape of my body. I've been forced to adopt a more sedentary lifestyle. There are days when I wish I could go back to where I was back then.

SHANE EDWARD LEE

After the navy discharged me, and I was let out of the hospital, I stayed in Virginia near to the base. I wanted to hang around there because it was somewhere I had grown to have an affinity to, even if it had soured by the end. It was also somewhere that wasn't Georgia. It was foreign to me, and I didn't want to close that chapter of my life quite yet and return to my home state and home town.

I stayed there until March 1996, when I eventually packed in the Virginia dream and moved home. It had gotten too hard in Virginia. Little things kept reminding me of my unhappiness and the accident, and I thought I should make a clean break and come back to the home that I knew and the support network of people that remained. They were few in number, but they were helpful all the same.

I tried to get into the construction business but then decided to move away from that and got a job at Little Caesar's Pizza, working in preparing the pizzas for customers and on the front counter. It was something I knew, but there was something wrong. Since the accident I had slowed down a step. It hurt to move, and in the cramped kitchen at Little Caesar's I had to twist and turn my leg too much. Eventually I got too slow for the owner, and had to go back into construction. I tried being a driver for the company, but my car quickly broke down and without that I was worse than useless to them, so they let me go. I got a job at a motel, doing menial stuff. This was the sort of life I was given after the navy: careening from one dead-end job to another. It was a test, sent to try me, and I kept up with it and constantly looked for something better. I went back to Labor Finders, and would get the same sort of bad jobs time and time again.

I found one which I liked after a while. I worked for an auto painting store called Stafford's Auto Paint in Savannah, GA. I was there for close to seven months working as a delivery driver for them. I would take the repainted cars that we had done work on and drive them wherever their owners were so they could pick them up, or I would mix the paint for our sister stores and deliver it to them. It was fun, because you'd get to drive all these different kinds of cars and although you had to be careful with them because they'd just had a paint job, altogether it was relatively stress free. I made a good $6.00 an hour, which wasn't bad pay. The people there were nice too. They told me there had been a nice Asian girl who worked there before I arrived, and one guy was even so nice as to tell me I could be a model.

The reason I had to leave was just a slight blip on the whole seven months of happiness. Our regular warehouse guy left and I was going to step into the breach and do his job, but after a short while we realized I couldn't because of my disabilities. A guy named Floyd came to work for us to replace our old warehouse guy. Everything was fine at first, and Floyd and I got on okay. But then we had a problem. We got into a fight in the warehouse – I don't remember what over – and he took a swing at me. He hit me on the mouth. I took a swing at him, and hit him square on the nose. After that it became untenable. I tried to get along with him, but certain types of men just take a dislike to you and show it, and in the end he refused to work with me so I had to leave. I was in pain every day – constantly – and the problems with Floyd were the last straw. I couldn't handle the mental pressure and discomfort on top of the mental ones.

Before that I was beginning to get back on track. I bought a cheap Ford Tempo to get back and forth to work, and would use that – and the freedom to travel that it afforded me – to catch up with people I hadn't seen for a while. I would travel up to see David Pellum at Steak Out, where he worked, and we would catch up and relive past memories like we were still 15. Sadly, though, the pain got too much and I had to quit there. I was still having tremendous trouble with my leg: I'd get shooting pains up and down it, and wouldn't be able to bear any weight on it at all. It was a nightmare. All I wanted to do was put the past behind me and get on with my life, but ill health and illness kept blighting my chance to move on.

I had filed with the Veterans Association as soon as I quit, and figured that I would get back paid from when I was discharged up to then, so I wasn't worried about not having an income. I was wrong. I was told that I had a year from my discharge to file my case with the VA to get disability payments. I was a few months late trying to reopen my case. I was honestly never told that I had to reopen my case within a year; I swear and affirm it. What else can I say? Either they refused to believe me, or simply didn't want to, or maybe they thought they could use my disability as a reason to not pay me. I don't know. No-one told me any different than what I believed the time period was. Had they told me any different, I would've done that. All I know is that it made it a hard time between the months I stopped working and the time my diminished disability payments started coming in. It was a hard fight to get them at all. I made less than $7,000 both years that I worked (1996 and 1997). That's not nearly enough to live on!

I was spit out into the world by the navy, and couldn't cope. I could barely make payments on my rent and bills. That's the whole point as to why I need the Veterans Association disability money. I need to make it through this world like everyone else, and I'm in debt. It's common decency: I've served my country. Luckily, during my service I wasn't called up to duty. But I still served my country all the same. Had 9/11 happened a few years earlier, then I would've been a member of the active military personnel on the front line. Sometimes I think that because I didn't go to war, the VA discriminate against me.

I went to a psychiatrist to try and sort out the payments by getting him to prove that I was disabled mentally, and he told me that even though I was schizophrenic I could work, even though one doctor told them I should be at least 50 to 70% disabled. They only gave me a 10% disability on my pelvis and ankle injury. I think that was a cover-up. I am way more than 10% disabled following my fall. Had I not been more than 10% injured, I would've had less problems. I've tried since to get the VA to raise my injured percentage to 100% so I can get the full payments I deserve.

They covered up a lot of my injuries. I'm certain that there were more broken bones than they said. I was having problems walking, standing and sitting. That's way more than 10% disabilities – I'm sure.

I got my disability payments starting from mid-1998. Right before then things were really difficult money and health wise. I managed to get heatstroke in April 1998, and was suffering from that while trying to finalize the details of my payments with the VA. All around this time the movie The Sphere, which had just come out a couple of months before, was playing in my head. It was horrendous.

In the movie, a navy team has to investigate a spaceship which crashes in the Pacific Ocean. It's fairly horrific. It starred Dustin Hoffman, Samuel L Jackson and Sharon Stone. All the time while I was trying to go about with my life, this was playing in my head, and I was part of it. The alien wreaks havoc on the crew tasked to find out what it is – in fact, it's not an alien at all. It's a United States ship. In it, when you reach the world of the perfect sphere, all your worst nightmares plague your mind and become reality. This was happening to me.

I desperately wanted a girlfriend. Someone who would understand me and help me through this difficult time was vital, I reasoned. I asked God to bring me someone as beautiful as Melissa Joan-Hart, who was in Sabrina the Teenage Witch at the time, which was a very good show. I knew that I had to wait on the dream woman to come to me, or I had to go and find her. That resulted in the episode where I was arrested by the police walking up the road naked.

I reckoned I had to show God I wasn't afraid. I went deep into my mind, and thought that I needed to be naked and unashamed at his coming (because it was seven years – an important number – since the start of the unrest in the Persian Gulf area which kicked off my problems) and prove that I was ready to meet Him in the air. I took off all my clothes – to show I wasn't afraid – and I walked up the street. Someone must've called the cops, because they turned up and I got into trouble. I was treated, though; they took me to the hospital, and I got better within two weeks.

I think it's important to say here that if you suffer from mental problems, you need to get help as soon as you think it's getting too much. Always, always when I was having medical problems, I would seek help. I'd go to the VA and tell them what was going on, or when I was in the navy I'd go straight to the hospital. You owe it to yourself and to other people to make sure someone knows about the problems and to get help for them as soon as possible. Otherwise they pile up and become worse, and you could end up hurting yourself or people around you. That's just about the last thing you want.

I had other run-ins with the law, too. I was falsely arrested on a bank robbery charge, right in the middle of my bluest period. The police came to my house and arrested me. They wouldn't let me explain myself – that I would never rob a bank. They said I looked like the person who robbed the bank. Someone, it turns out, had wandered into a branch of the Wachovia Bank in Georgia and drained them of my money. I used my common sense here (and tried to parlay it into proving to the VA that I was not as psychologically damaged as they said I was, while also proving I was very disabled physically): I said that first off, I could not possibly have been able-bodied enough to be able to pull off a bank heist. Mentally, I demonstrated to the VA that I knew the difference between good and bad. I would never rob a bank: I knew that it was bad.

I had to go on Social Security until my disabled money came through in 1999. I did get *a little* back pay, though it wasn't enough to cover my bills or anything. I decided to use the little money I was given through the VA at the time as a lump sum to try and invest for the future. I bought two cars: one was a yellow 1998 Mustang, and the other was a 1996 Nissan King Cab. My eventual aim was that one day I could give one of the cars to my son, Jonathan Rowen Sebastian Lee, as a bequeathal when he was old enough to drive. I wanted him to be able to explore the open roads in the way that I too often couldn't. I wanted him to be able to get out of there.

I wrote to my Congressman and the local Senators about my treatment. I was on a crusade. I thought it was a double standard for the military to be on a different level than the civilian government. I thought that it was unfair that a veteran couldn't have two whole years to reopen his or her claim if they filed it right away. I felt like I was being handicapped because I tried to work (because of the low disability rating the VA gave me). I got so annoyed that I wrote to President Bush, and posted a couple of comments on the Congress website to try and get them to change the law to so that I can get compensated right back to when I was discharged rather than when I filed the claim. I think it's an important right, because I believe it was the navy which gave me the disability. The fight is a fight which I've continued to this day with the Veterans Association. They still refuse to offer me the full backdated pay that I believe I am entitled to, but I won't stop fighting for it. They've broken me too much for me not to fight for it.

I kept myself busy. I used to find occasional work; odd jobs really, but enough to give me a few bucks. I couldn't work full-time – I couldn't possibly work full-time, because of the pain and because I was taking David back and forth to work, helping him out. He was having a busy time: he had a daughter with his current girlfriend and two daughters with his ex-wife (to whom he was behind on child support payments). I helped him get his driving license back (he'd lost it earlier) and get him a job at Gulfstream, who make the jets. I even lost my two cars to help him get his own: that's how charitable I was.

I wanted to add David to the insurance of my Nissan King Cab so he could use it. I would keep my Mustang and just use that. He wouldn't hear any of it. That was too much, he said. But I wanted to help him nonetheless. So I traded out my Nissan and my Mustang for a Ford Taurus SHO V8. It was black with chrome wheels. I took David along to the showroom, and made him get a blue Daytona Dodge V-6. I think it was a 1992 model – he was so proud. I co-signed for him on his Dodge – at least that was the plan. It all got messed up. It turned out that both cars were now in my name because of some mistake at the dealership.

I was able – just – to make payments on the Taurus, but David couldn't keep up his payments on the Dodge. I had to trade out of my Taurus and get a 2000 Dodge Stratus, which I upgraded later to a 2003 Dodge Neon, while David defaulted on his payments, wrecked his Dodge and got it repossessed. He thought it was all going to be on my insurance, but by that point I had taken him off. He tried to blame me a little bit for that, thinking it was a sneaky move, but look at it from my perspective: I had helped him out enormously. I *still* helped him out. I was still doing what I could, but I was struggling myself. I couldn't afford to pay for the upkeep of two cars and to pay insurance on them both – especially when one of them wasn't even mine.

Eventually David moved out of state with his girlfriend, but through it all and despite him souring on our relationship a bit towards the end I kept a positive attitude towards him. I hope he's well.

Around this time I read the Bible four different ways. I had already read it from 1996-1998 when part of the Christian Fellowship Church International, but I wanted to read it properly and to delve into the detail it provided. I wanted to get closer to God – a task a lot of people want – and so I thought I would devote myself to fully understanding the Bible, cover to cover.

I got an interlinear Bible in both Hebrew and Greek, and Strong's Concordance which I've already mentioned, which opened up the Bible to even more interpretation. I started learning. I wanted to keep myself as busy as possible through the arthritic pain, the scar tissue damage and all the mental problems. When I was working I would go to sleep at night with tears in my eyes from all the pain, but I'd get up the following morning all the same and turn out for work wherever they'd have me.

I bounced from job to job. I drove for Kathryn Stevens for a couple of months, then worked service at KFC for a month or so. I worked part-time at the local movie theater called the Westside Cinemas. That started out really well: I was working plenty of hours and doing well, and my bosses were pleased. But like before, the middle of my back, by left femur and hip joint and my ankle would begin to ache and bother me to the point where I couldn't stand, sit or walk for long periods. I felt like I was becoming old before my old age.

I would go home and rest and recuperate, and would get back to working fitness, but the cycle repeated itself. As soon as I found a good job where they liked me, my injuries would come back to haunt me and I would be forced to stop for my own health. I was particularly promising at Cooper Tires in Garden City, GA. I started off full-time, and for the first week I was fine. In fact, I was more than fine: I did so well that they wanted to hire me. True to form, by the second week my back and arthritic pain kicked in, and

I slowed down a lot. Their initial impressions wilted to disappointment. I got into a car crash where the airbag didn't deploy, which caused more suffering and pain. All I got for that accident was $3,000 from the insurance company.

I got my first computer a while back and got myself connected to the internet at the same time. It was April 2004, and it was a Compaq I got from the computer store. I decided at the time to get a webcam to go with it, and the sales assistant recommended a Logitec webcam as they were a trusted brand, so I bought that separately. I was so excited when I got it all home and set it up, because it opened up a whole new world of opportunity and information to explore. Like most people, I signed up for the internet with AOL, though I've since moved to Comcast. I realized even back then that there is an awful lot of bad stuff out there on the internet: it's par for the course when it comes to such an unregulated morass of information, I suppose. Some of my early internet searches were tentative and as befits the time back then, they often turned up some unexpected results. I wasn't enormously keen on some of the things my web browser dealt me, but what it did was ignite zeal in me to counteract the bad with some good. For all that it is extraordinarily easy to upload and disseminate something unwholesome and morally corrupting on the internet to an audience that would in the past have never experienced it, it is just as easy to gain an audience for something good. That's what I decided to do. A statistic I've read said that there are millions of porn websites out there. I was determined to beat on against the current to try and return to a more innocent past.

I started out on the internet by creating a website from which I could spread the word of God; to explain to any personal readers things in the Bible that other men wouldn't look upon, because they don't believe that they are worthy enough to understand what the scriptures say. I was hoping to democratize the practice of religion, and to help affirm their faith in doing so. It was also me acting out against the navy and Veteran's Association that I was capable of doing something with my life and learning something new, despite the problems I had with my fellow shipmates.

They were big goals, but started with simple words. Early on the morning of Tuesday, 10 May 2005 – the records show it was 1:29am – I wrote my first blog. I started it well before midnight the day before, and committed to electrons my thoughts and feelings on the Bible, and how I had been blessed. I believed then (as I believe now) that I am one of God's two witnesses, so the title of my first blog post on the Angelfire website I started was 'One of the two witnesses'. I was reading about the two witnesses mentioned in the Book of Revelation, and heard a voice say "that's you." The first blog was a simple, humble beginning, setting out (as I have done in an extended version here on paper) who I am, what had happened to me, and what I wanted to do for others. "Hello to all of you who are seeking the truth of God," it began. "My name is Shane Lee and I have been studying the Bible since I was a child, and have read it over 5 times, and would like to share need to know information." I opened up my heart, and continued for just short of 12,000 words. I closed it purposefully, with a declaration of intent: "I testify that all of the information contained in this blog is true to the best of my knowledge and or belief."

I can't pretend that the website took off enormously, but it had some readers. That's what the internet is like: it's a great democratizing movement, which allows the little guy's voice to be heard at an equal level to the big guy's. Anyone can set up a website, a blog, or a Youtube account online (unless you're in a nation which decides that they don't want to promote free speech but rather stifle the internet – and truthfully, that seems to me to be a pointless process because the internet is so broad, so big and so all-encompassing that it's almost impossible to put a leash on it) and broadcast it to anyone who is interested enough to pay attention. It's a great idea, and it allowed me to show people that you don't need to be a pastor, or to have gone to church school, or have consulted with religious higher-ups in order to interpret and spread the word of the scriptures. I'm not against churches – even the ones that did me wrong. They're great for a base understanding of the Bible, for a starting point, but they don't go into enough detail. They gloss over the bits which truly help understand the power of the Lord, and anything that might be considered even slightly unsavory. I had read the Bible, truly studying it, since I was a child, sure, and by that point had read it cover to cover over five times. But I was a lay person: I wasn't a pastor, I wasn't a priest. I was just someone who believed in God, and believed that I was put on the earth to spread the word of God.

"I will give power unto my two witnesses, and they shall prophesy a thousand two hundred and threescore days, clothed in sackcloth", it says in Revelation 11:3. I was here to prophesy the word of God to the world, all clothed in sackcloth, and to tell that that through my adversity – my sackcloth – that things could and would get better if you followed the path of Jesus. I decided to do this online. I decided to use my personal website; later, I decided to use Youtube.

For now, though, my Angelfire website was sufficient.

The whole purpose behind it was to unpick the Bible so that ordinary people could understand it. In Ancient Greece – in Delphi, in particular, the great city-state which was built deep into the natural contours of the high mountains of Parnassus around it so that nature provided an insurmountable defense – they were famous for their prophecies and soothsayers. Delphi had its oracle, and people would travel from miles around to consult it. They would bring their sick and dying, their meek and troubled, and they would approach the temple at Delphi and ask the oracle what would happen to them. They would ask if their future looked bright or dark; if they could have a triumphant marriage or a failed one. They would ask anything and everything to the oracle.

The problem was that the oracle was hidden from view, deep in the bowels of the temple, beyond the gleaming marble face. People would come to question Apollo, and would not be able to do so themselves. The Pythia, who was an old woman, pure of heart, would sit on a tripod above a crack in the temple and interpret the signs she was given by Apollo. Her interpretation would be in strange tongues, screaming and thrashing, and people would be scared. The priests gathered in the temple would translate her screaming into the Greek that the visitors to the temple would understand, and so the oracle at Delphi was passed on to lay people.

I am like the priests at the temple. God is Apollo, and the Pythia are those scribes who committed the Bible to paper. I translate that which is deemed untranslatable by ordinary people; I make the impenetrable penetrable. That's what I believe is my task, and it's what I am to do online. Isaiah 29:11 says "and the vision of all is become unto you as the words of a book that is sealed, which men deliver to one that is learned, saying, Read this, I pray thee: and he saith, I cannot; for it is sealed."

It's my belief that there are passages in the Bible that men won't teach to other men, either through willing compulsion or for some less suspicious reason. A lot of the time, interpreters of the Bible hold back true interpretation of some passages from the people they're informing because they believe that they are unworthy to understand the truth, and it's something I find infuriating and confusing. The entire Bible was written to be read and understood, as well as disseminated. To cherry pick sections seems pointless to me. You either tell everyone it all, or you tell them nothing. Without an encyclopedic knowledge of the Bible, you can't possibly pretend to use it as a guide. It would be like reading half this book, then declaring yourself an expert on my life. Likewise, you wouldn't read half of a manual on how to operate nuclear weapons, then believe that you can be trusted to be in control of pushing the button to unleash them on someone were the time to come when that was necessary. In some situations, knowing as little as possible can be useful: Malcolm Gladwell, a great thinker who writes for *The New Yorker*, wrote as much in a book he released called *Blink*. He had a theory of 'thin slicing', where our gut instincts are often the best when it comes to certain things. If you add in too many variables of candy bar, for example, we can stand in the candy aisle for half an hour and weigh up the benefits of each candy bar: whether they have nougat, a lack of raisins, the quantity of chocolate we're getting and so on, and can come out at the end with an unsatisfying bar of candy. In situations like that, our first gut instinct would've been the best driver. If we wanted a Milky Way, we should've got the Milky Way and not considered that perhaps the Almond Joy might give us more value for money. There, thin slicing works. In things like understanding the Bible (a complex and confusing book which forms the basis of an entire theological belief and acts as the pillar of numerous civilizations – and has done for centuries) to be better prepared is always best. You almost certainly cannot know enough about the Bible; you definitely can't know too much.

I therefore see myself as the people's pastor, being unflinching in my recounting of the Bible, good and bad, just as I'm unflinching in my recounting of my life, even though large parts of it might reflect badly on me or my religion. I'm not going to shy away from telling people how my pastor tried to molest me, simply because it would not fit in with the grand narrative of how all religion is good and all those involved in spreading religion are pious and without sin.

In fact, I challenge other pastors. I ask them this directly: are you teaching the whole truth of God, or just the parts of it that you think are sufficient to get your congregation into heaven? Teaching them part-way might get them part-way there, but only by teaching every word from the scriptures can you be assured that your congregation isn't devoured by the Evil One.

Most pastors withhold the truth in unrighteousness, even though they may be trying to be good in the process of doing so. Though they follow the obvious commandments laid out in the Bible, they tempt God and taunt him in their shirking of teaching the others. You need to get at the deeper things; superficial learning of the Bible leads to tempting God, which is what homosexuals do: they hold the truth in unrighteousness, and treat it as shades of gray rather than a binary thing. You have to either tell someone everything, or you may as well not tell them anything at all.

There are two types of knowledge to my mind: knowledge that you get from knowing your environment, and all those around you, and knowledge that there is something greater than you out there. When it comes to the latter, I've found it a great comfort to know that the something greater than me – God – loves me and wants me to prosper in the world that He created for me to live in. It's comforting to me, and I want to give other people that comfort and safety net of knowing that there is someone greater. Thus I came up with the website. It's all well and good having the *intention* of telling people about God, but you have to actually be proactive and put the information out there. Even though through my website I was not actively going up to people and thrusting the word of God onto them – a tactic which can have its drawbacks, as cold calling and techniques like that can in fact drive people away rather than lure them towards something – I was putting the information out there, so anyone who was interested in learning more and had the basic knowledge of a search engine like Google could find it. One of my favorite films is *Wayne's World 2*: it's really funny, a tale about two goofy guys who have a dream and eventually become less slovenly than they are at the start of the movie and start up a rock festival. It's pretty popular, so I'm sure you've seen it, or at least heard of it and the plot. In *Wayne's World 2* there is a famous quote – one that almost everyone I've met knows – which I use to justify why I built the website and put up the blogs on it when I did, and which I use to demonstrate why I continue to use Youtube and various other sites to put up videos and information. The quote, the mantra that they use when they create their rock festival is "if you build it, they will come."

People did come and read my blogs; in the first I was purely telling people about my religious faith and why I believe it is important. For example, I wrote in the first blog way back in May 2005 about the all-encompassing importance of the Bible: all the writings in the Old and New Testament (every last word of them) were to prepare people for the messenger of the covenant who was going to come into the earth in the form of a woman and attempt to redeem men from the original sin in Eden. My purpose in writing the blogs, I said then (and still believe now, even though it has extended to my Youtube videos and tweets) was and is to empower people by giving them the knowledge of God to overcome Satan in their lives. It's a physical and a psychological battle, and it's not easy. I see myself as one of the two witnesses from the Book of Revelation who is chosen to explain the seven seals.

A lot of people can see my point in this, and agree with me. But just as many ask an obvious question: Shane, why do you use Youtube to post videos of you singing (the video of me singing the five octaves on piano has hundreds of thousands of Youtube hits and has spawned numerous spin-off videos, for example) or wishing people Happy Birthday or performing impersonations or comedy?

My answer to that is simple: if I were to only upload boring sermons about religion, I would not have as many viewers, and therefore my more pertinent religious points would not be seen by as many people. You have to lure people in with light entertainment in order to ensure they take in the information you really want them to. For example, television networks will often put some of their highest-rating shows on just before some of their lowest. The aim is to get eyeballs in front of shows which aren't doing so well, in the hope that the audience will be exposed to something they ordinarily wouldn't watch. It's the same with me and my videos: if someone comes to my Youtube channel and they're a fan of the Beatles, they may well be irreligious drug takers. However, if they watch me singing the song 'Help' by the Beatles, then when the video is over, they click on a related video which explains why God is great, then perhaps they will be exposed to something new which they wouldn't ordinarily have considered, and it may change their perception of Christianity. It's all about providing a hook for people to take: once they grab the bait, and subscribe to you, you can guide them towards other videos you create that tell a more wholesome story.

It's why Sunday schools choose to teach kids about the stories from the Bible with songs and humor; it's why I use comedy in my videos. By putting a four-minute digest of my Biblical studies on Youtube after I've sung 'You Sexy Thing', for example, people are more likely to find it accessible and fun than reading 12,000 words I've written in a blog. You have to adapt to the situation you find yourself in and try and provide the most suitable and popular way to get ahead. In this case, it's by couching religious matters in humor and pop music. A lot of professional pastors won't do that: they're resolutely stuck in the old ways, preaching to the already-converted and not growing their congregation. I have a constantly expanding group of viewers and subscribers, most of who are incredibly loyal and are open to my religious videos. They're my congregation. And I'm thankful for them.

I started my Youtube account two years after I first got the computer, and one year after I started up my website on Angelfire, in May 2006. My first video was called 'Hello to the Youtube community', and offered a short introduction to me and my life and what I wanted to do with the videos I was going to upload. You can't find that video anymore, because the account it was uploaded on – along with nearly 400 other early videos – was deleted because I cussed on a video. I said the world "motherfucker" on one video, and someone reported it, and they deleted my account and everything that was on it. I stuck with Youtube though, and set up a separate account, and was careful in the future to make sure that my videos weren't lewd and abided by their terms and conditions.

I was nervous, making that first video. Though you're only broadcasting in real time to your webcam, there is a potential audience of millions out there, and it's that which really gets to you. The potential of the internet is tremendous, and so you really feel (or at least I do feel) the gravity of the situation, and the weight of people that could at any time log on to Youtube and watch your video. You have a need to be entertaining and informative, and as I'm pretty sure everyone knows the internet can be the harshest critics of material.

I've had my fair share of critics, too. It's a byproduct of the internet, the anonymising quality that the internet has. You can shroud yourself in a separate body, almost – and certainly in a different mind. The internet, and its anonymity, allows people to unleash a more amplified version of themselves; it allows people to turn up the viciousness they feel towards others, which might otherwise go unexpressed in real life when you have to be face-to-face with the person you're talking to, and it allows them to say what they want without fear of repercussions.

Trolling is what it's called online. Deliberately antagonizing people – often those who are defenseless or particularly vulnerable – is just part and parcel of being online. You don't like it, sure, but you have to get on with it. If you're willing to put yourself out there, you have to be willing to take the flak which will inevitably come your way when someone doesn't like you, or they decide that regardless of what they think of you, they want to make your life a living hell.

Trolling runs completely opposite to my line of thinking: I want to see the best in everybody and accentuate the positives. It's why I believe that I need to spread the joy and the happiness of God to as many people as I can. But I know that there are people out there on the internet who take joy in causing misery, and I know that I have to weather their barbs in order to be able to put across my message to the overwhelming majority of positive supporters that I have.

There is a website called Encyclopedia Dramatica which is a humor website which specializes in making fun of people. It's like an anti-Wikipedia; it says that white people are an inferior race, and you're supposed to find humor in the dichotomy between perception and fact. It's funny because white people don't generally have a problem with racism, while black people are often faced with the most horrific forms of racism and just get on with it. White people complain, but they don't have those sorts of problems. That's the sort of humor that Encyclopedia Dramatica has.

I have an entry on it. I don't know who created it, and I don't know who edits it, but there I am. At the top of the page the last time I visited it (because of the nature of a Wiki, it may well have changed by the time you take a look) is a banner saying "FAT ALERT". "Shane Lee is fat. Go ahead and tell him!", with a link to my Youtube video. It's not a very pleasant entry. They write that I have "wonderful talents," which would be lovely except that it's probably sarcasm. You realize that as you read on. "His followers cheer him on, and fill his empty head with the idea that he has the makings of greatness. This points to what kind of people [here they link to the definition page of 'Faggots'] those fans are. It's kind of hurtful, what they write, but you have to accept it, because it's the internet and some people get their kicks from ruining other people's day.

They quote some people on there who claim that I'm a stalker. I personally think they are. Two guys on the internet decided to follow me around and unpick my fragile mental state and claim things that aren't true, like I'm lying about my disability or that I stalk women or that I molest children. None of that is true, but because it's the internet, they're entitled to an equal hearing. They have – or had – a vendetta against me, and decided that they wanted to try and ruin my reputation while all I wanted to do was spread the word of the scriptures and put light into people's lives. Two people created Youtube accounts, hiding behind false names (ShaneLeeTheFraudToo and shameONYOUshane) at about the same time in 2007. They quoted me out of context, portraying it like I was saying bad things.

For example, one of them has a quote from me, supposedly from October 16, 2009, saying "I was a stalker, temporarily." They have taken me totally out of context. But that's what you have to expect on the internet: people have irrational hatred of others, borne out of nothing at all, which they pursue constantly.

They have even trawled through my records from the Navy Medical Board and quoted them out of context too! shameONYOUshane posted nine textual points and five videos (nothing else is on his profile, showing that he is in fact a psychopathic stalker – the very thing he accuses me of) all trying to belittle me. I've quoted his nine points below and refute them, point by point:

POST ONE:

Hey everyone! Let's READ THE TRUTH

about Sham E. Lee... right from his official

Navy Medical Board FINDINGS.

I quote:

"He DROPPED OUT of High School with

BELOW AVERAGE GRADES. He had

REPEATED 6th and 11th GRADES DUE TO

EXCESSIVE ABSENCES. he stated that his favorite subject or activity was "studying the Bible". He endorsed neuropathic traits of childhood, INCLUDING ANIMAL CRUELTY AND STEALING. He held several FAST FOOD JOBS prior to enlistment".

I did repeat sixth grade, and 11th grade too, because of excessive absences. As you will know, reader, from reading this autobiography, at the time I was struggling with serious mental illnesses and traumatic events that were happening in my life. You'll know, from the timeline that I've presented to you, that sixth grade was right around the time my dad died. I have to ask you: would you not find it difficult to concentrate on schoolwork if your father had been shot dead while you were shopping? Would you not be bothered about attending school while you were mourning? I didn't cry at the funeral, but that doesn't mean that I wasn't hurting.

As to my favorite subject being studying the Bible, I fail to see what is wrong with that. I was demonstrating my strong faith in religion, and I would rather that my favorite activity was that than something less honest or wholesome.

Likewise, I don't understand why working several jobs, even if they are "FAST FOOD JOBS" is such a bad thing. Many people come out of school and never get a job, and instead choose to take benefits. I was working, earning a wage and contributing to the economy. The fact that I was working prior to enlisting with the navy is, if anything, a positive thing. I wanted to work to pay my way through life.

Finally, I defy you to find any child who has not stolen or entertained the thought of stealing. Like I've said before, anything I stole was petty theft, like the pennies from my uncle, and I have repented for my sins and admitted that it was wrong. It shows me to be a good person to be able to admit to my failings in such a public manner and to show remorse for them.

POST TWO:

"He went to CAPTAIN'S MAST ONE TIME, FOR SLEEPING ON WATCH. His evaluations averaged 2.8 and he (Sham Lee) characterized his (own) military performance as "AWFUL"

I was really tired the night that I fell asleep, which again is not a crime. I was sent to Captain's Mast and I knew I had done wrong and I was punished for it. I admitted to the sergeant at the time of the evaluation that I had done "awful" at the task, which was me being honest. Would the navy (and the person who created the shameONYOUshane) account rather I was unrealistic about my performance and delusionally said that I was brilliant?

POST THREE:

"Following a review of the clinical findings, the Medical Board is of the opinion that the

patient is unfit for military service AS A
RESULT OF A CONDITION THAT EXISTED
PRIOR TO HIS ENLISTMENT and is
considered to have incurred in or to have
been aggravated by a period of active duty.
The Medical Board is further of the opinion
that the member fails to fulfill the
minimum standards for enlistment OR
INDUCTION, as set forth in the Manual of
the Medical Department, Chapter 15."

I fail to see how this is a negative thing against me. I have always said that I had a condition – paranoid schizophrenia – prior to admission to the navy, which was made worse by duty. I tried out for the navy, and was accepted because I had managed to achieve well during enlistment. I was then subject to systematic abuse by my fellow shipmates, who never gave me a chance to assimilate. This aggravated my condition, and meant that I was unable to perform to the best of my abilities, because my mind was occupied with trying to figure out why my shipmates had taken such a disliking to me.

POST FOUR:
"He noticed NO EFFECT from medication
and DISCONTINUED IT HIMSELF after his
discharge from the hospital. The Medical
Board granted him ZERO PERCENT
DISABILITY based on THEIR FINDING OF

EXISTENCE PRIOR TO ENTRY STATUS OF
THE DIAGNOSIS" - National Naval Medical
Center, Department of Psychiatry,
Inpatient Division, Bethesda Maryland -
Medical Board Addendum"

It's true that I didn't feel any positive effects from
the medication I was given, so I took myself off
it. I believe that it exacerbated my condition and
made me worse, which would not have been
beneficial to me or others.

POST FIVE:
SUMMARY -

The previous 4 posts contain data from the
official Medical Board who examined Sham
Lee. This is the information SHAM
WITHHELD from the VA, which would
have resulted in his disability being
rightfully denied.
Sham Lee had PRE-EXISTING mental issues
which he FAILED TO DISCLOSE at the time
of induction that if disclosed would have
prevented him from being inducted.
He lied to get into the Navy. He
characterized his own service as "AWFUL".

I believed that I could perform in the navy when
I applied to be in it. I was never asked by the

Veterans Association for the information that this person has posted online when applying for disability benefit. I'm pleased and proud to be able to call myself a disabled veteran, even though my spell in the navy – to my mind at least – made my existing condition worse.

POST SIX:

SUMMARY CONT'D –

Sham was a high school dropout, who had a history of ANIMAL CRUELTY and STEALING; both of which are common traits of sociopathy in youth. Sham had no skills prior to enlistment. After enlistment, he violated direct and general orders, stalked women, malingered, failed to do his job, fell asleep on watch during wartime, and generally failed to honorably do his service.

This all seems to be repeating information which I have previously shown to be untrue or false, or taken out of context. I did have skills prior to my enlistment in the navy: I have a GED and as I've explained in the passages in this autobiography relating to my childhood, I was particularly good at karate, getting a blue belt, which is only two away from the prestigious black belt.

POST SEVEN:

SUMMARY CONT'D:

Sham Lee had 2.8 evaluations which by Navy standards, are considered SUBSTANDARD. In the Navy, 4.0 is perfect and 3.6 is AVERAGE. Sham Lee had 2.8, which are so low, they justify involuntary discharge on their own merit. If you have a heartbeat... and show up for work, you will get at least a 3.4. At 2.8, it is clear that Sham Lee made every effort to not serve in an honorable fashion

Sham Lee is an admitted liar. he lied to get in the Navy, and he lied to the VA

The notion that "if you have a heartbeat...and show up for work, you will get at least a 3.4" is patently untrue because I have a heartbeat and did show up for work but did not. The scale is a sliding scale, from 0 to 4. I got a 2.8. That wasn't great, but it wasn't the worst possible.

The notion that I was dishonorable is hurtful and obviously not true, given that I try to live my life in every aspect in as honorable a way as possible, including admitting freely my own faults and failures to those who will listen. My openness is refreshing in a world where people are willing to turn first to lies and obfuscations, rather than the truth, no matter how badly it may portray you.

There follows another two points which sum up the person's arguments (or I should say lack of arguments) and challenge and threaten me:

POST EIGHT:

SUMMARY CONCLUSION -

So people... now that you can see Sham Lee is a liar and is bilking the system for money on fraudulent grounds, DO SOMETHING ABOUT IT!

Go to vadotgovslashoig and DEMAND a FRAUD INVESTIGATION against Shane Edward Lee of Garden City, GA (257-23-2433). Tell the Inspector General to review Shane Lee's Navy Medical Records and Personnel files for the Medical Board FIndings and addendum, which Sham Lee failed to provide to the VA.

HELP REAL INJURED VETS!

So, Sham E. Lee... what have you got to say for yourself, you animal abusing, thieving, flunk-out, dropout, burger flipper? Still think you served "honorably", with your below-average school grades, way below average Naval evaluations, Non-Judicial

> **Punishments, and history of lack of**
>
> **performance? Still think that people buy**
>
> **your crap... when it is clear that are an**
>
> **admitted liar who lied to get in the Navy**
>
> **and now lies to get a free paycheck?**
>
> **Once a liar, always a liar.**
>
> **We don't buy your lies.**

In a way, this is just a continuation of the reception I was given by my shipmates in the navy. In fact, it's a similar reception to that I got in school. It's why I have so many problems – problems which I freely admit to. Psychological trauma can come from the words and actions of other human beings. To trolls on the internet, it may seem like they are just having fun and that there are no consequences. However there are real consequences to actions. Having to fend off the allegations that people make online (both from casual trolls who like to try and rile me up in the comments sections of my videos and from more persistent stalkers like shameONYOUshane and ShaneTheFraudToo) means I cannot put as much work as I would like into my rehabilitation and trying to make myself better.

ShaneLeeTheFraudToo does a similar thing to shameONYOUshane with their Youtube profile, this time quoting me, rather than my medical board findings, out of context.

For example, I once said that I can function up to 4 or 6 hours a day if things are well, but that it is difficult – if not impossible – to find an employer who is willing to take someone with mental health issues on for such a small daily amount of time. Unless someone from the entertainment community, where hours are generally less and the work is physically less strenuous (also a problem given my physical frailty) is willing to help me out somehow, it seems unlikely that I will ever find gainful employment. This admission of a problem suddenly became, through the eyes of this one-track stalker, me "taking the bread out of the mouth [sic] of you and your children" because I choose not to work. Like I said above: I am willing to work for as long as I am able to. However, mitigating circumstances mean that the amount of time I can work, and the types of job I can do, are limited. That makes it difficult for an employer to employ me. I can't compel people to give me a job against their wishes. That's not how the world works.

Particularly hurtful to me is the idea that these people have and continually drive home to others that I somehow decided to jump off the roof when in the navy, and claim that I fell.

Why on earth would I risk death for what they perceive to be financial gain? I may have my problems, but I am not stupid enough to do that.

That's part of the problem with the internet: outlandish ideas can be given credence just because there are no checks and balances. Anyone can say anything, with pretty much no fear of repercussions. Reputations, like mine, can be slandered in an instant by someone who has just invented a grudge to keep them occupied through the day.

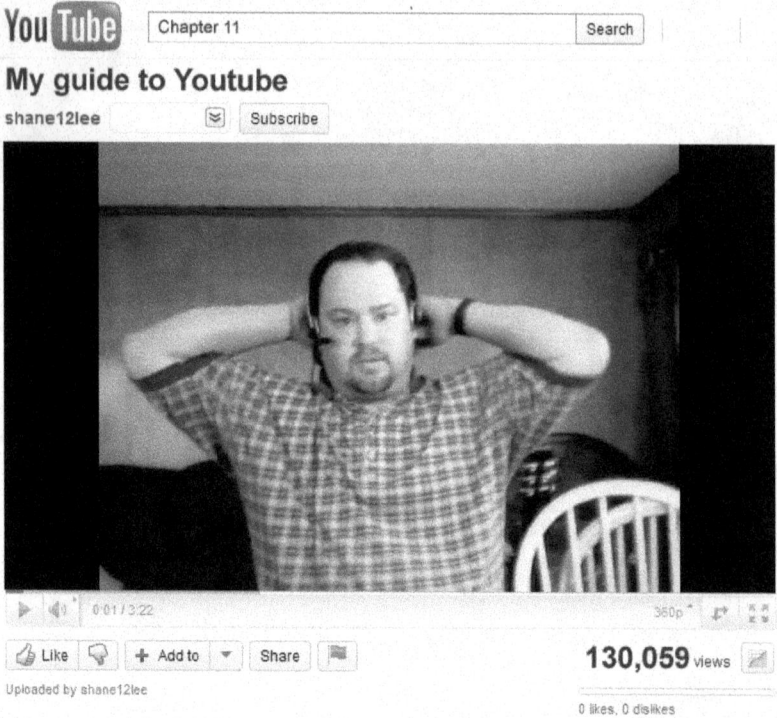

Chapter 11 ・ Search

My guide to Youtube

shane12lee ・ Subscribe

0:01 / 3:22 ・ 360p

Like ・ Add to ・ Share

Uploaded by shane12lee

130,059 views

0 likes, 0 dislikes

But enough about that. It's a bad idea to linger on the bad things; like it says in Philippians 4:8, "finally, brethren, whatsoever things are true, whatsoever things are honest, whatsoever things are just, whatsoever things are pure, whatsoever things are lovely, whatsoever things are of good report; if there be any virtue, and if there be any praise, think on these things."

Instead, I want to talk about my Youtube successes, and my tips on how to become a Youtube phenomenon.

In many ways, being a Youtube star is not much unlike being a television star. Glenn Beck was able to create an enormous public audience from the outrageous stuff that he said, backed up by his strength of convictions. At its peak, his Fox News show had 3 million viewers – a huge number for a program on a cable news channel. In fact, I see a lot of myself in Glenn Beck. Both of us had troublesome childhoods; both of us lost a parent at about the same time, and both of us have fallen off the wagon in the past, but managed to haul ourselves back on and try and make a respectable pass at life. For Glenn, it was his mother who he lost in a sailing accident that he believes was a suicide. For me, I lost my dad because a friend turned up one day and murdered him. Until you go through such troublesome, traumatic events in your childhood, you don't realize quite how much it affects your psyche.

Beck, by his own admission, is borderline schizophrenic – a condition which I have been medically diagnosed with – and has ADD. He has physical problems, too. He recently told people, just before his run on Fox News ended, that he had been diagnosed with "small fiber neuropathy". My physical problems prevent me from working; his seem less problematic, and he can work in the entertainment industry, where the hours and workload is less strenuous than manual labor.

He started small and made it big: ultimately, that is what I would like to do. He classes himself as a truth-teller, creating his own online university and magazine, while also touring around clubs and theatres as a comedian. My website and Youtube accounts are an attempt to profess the truth of the Bible, but I combine that with comedy and songs to try and get an audience.

It's that combination – the mixture of comedy and seriousness – which is key to being a Youtube success. If you take yourself too seriously, and produce long diatribes of you talking directly to the camera without any humor interspersed in amongst the facts, then no-one will watch. College-aged users are the most likely to visit Youtube. They do so because they want to escape their classes and switch off. They pay enough money already to hear from people with real accreditations and qualifications, Doctors and

Masters of their fields, talk about a certain subject. They don't need Joe Schmo trying to tell them something else in a dour accent. You need to spruce up your act, make it fun. The medium is the message, and no-one will listen to your message if you medium is boring.

I use songs and personal requests, as well as telling jokes, as an in for viewers. They come for those, and they stay for the more religious, earnest aspects of my videos. You're more likely to have an appreciative audience if you lighten the mood with a joke. People become more open to hearing what you have to say if they're put at ease; if they're made to laugh. People like nothing more than laughing. It's a natural human instinct. When you laugh, your stress levels lower and your trust levels rise. Humor is important to being a success on Youtube: when you think of the number of people out there, uploading videos 24 hours a day, seven days a week, you have to have something that sets you apart from the mass. You need to be funny, or quirky, or both. You need a schtick.

Glenn Beck realized that, which is why he tours around the country performing stand-up comedy. I would love to be able to do that. I could travel from state to state, performing comedy shows where I could do my impressions and sing, then talk about my journey through life and my redemption, and my faith in God. It wouldn't be all that different to Glenn Beck, and what he does.

What Glenn Beck also does is a televisual version of life blogging. Life blogging is big on Youtube: you have personalities that upload videos daily (or regularly, at least), telling their audience about their lives. At first, you might find that these life bloggers have very few viewers. But gradually, as their audience gets to know them, and as you become more engaged with the person in front of the lens, the numbers rise. Life bloggers are great talkers, and I consider myself to be one of life's great talkers. My aunt always said to me "Shane, you could talk the back leg off a mule!" It's important to be able to talk, because it's what we use to connect ourselves to other humans. When you stand in front of a camera and prepare to make a Youtube video, essentially what you're doing is talking to yourself in the hope that a large group of people will eventually be listening in. You need to have the gift to talk ceaselessly. That's why the most popular Youtube users are the most charismatic people: they can talk lots.

I once got asked as part of a question-and-answer series I did on Youtube with someone called Slice of Metal what I would do were I given a five to eight minute slot on-stage. It was simple, I told him.

I would come out and start out saying "hi everybody, how are you doing? Want to talk to you tonight about the situation in Tucson" (this was when Gabrielle Giffords was shot – I wouldn't just talk about Tucson every night. I might change this part up depending on what was happening in the news). "We know there's a tragedy there, but there's a very uplifting hope and spirit as people try and work out the difficulties of life."

I would try and point out the positives, even in the worst situations. That's what I'm like.

Then, I'd start out properly with some rockabilly – and I'd do my air rockabilly guitar and banjo – to get the audience warmed up. From there, I'd move on and explain that it's hard to talk to such a large audience (I'm only used to a small Youtube audience who are remote). I'd tell them I have their back, though. That's important.

It's all a moot point, though. I'm a Youtube person, not a stage star.

I see myself as a life blogger. I talk extensively online about my life; I've even written this, more than 50,000 words of autobiography on my life, to present to anyone who chooses to pay to read it. I think it helps people trust you, and makes them more willing to believe what you say. You're expecting (or you're hoping) people will give up their too precious free time to watch what you have to show them on Youtube, or to read your blog, so you have to give something back. It's not a one-way process: there is interaction. These people let you into their lives remotely; you have to let them into yours. Talking to them about your day, about your past, about work or about your love life or your dreams or expectations, your hopes and fears, all that is part of the give and take. You're winning them onside by telling them about your life; about your failings and your plus points. The personal experience you have can be parlayed into talking about your wider ideal: for me, I can explain how all the problems I went through as a kid girded me towards religion. I can say that the miracles that were me cheating death made me more fervent in my religious belief. I can use them as proof positive that God exists – because if He did not, then why would I be sitting there today in front of them on Youtube, and I can explain that through adversity and through all the problems, He has helped keep me positive and on track.

Glenn Beck has the same story to tell. Through his faith, he says, he is a "recovering dirtbag" – and I believe him. Now he's turned to the internet, using a fee-paying online television setup that's not all that dissimilar to Youtube. He already has the personality and the mix of humor and gravitas to make him a Youtube phenomenon. But if you want to be successful, you could do much worse than look at Glenn Beck and take notes.

I know what it's like to be an evangelist. I would often go into the community, wherever I was living, and teach right there on the spot. I would teach and preach in malls and shops, on street corners and sidewalks. What I do on Youtube is a natural extension of that: it's allowing me to reach a wider audience than I ever have before. In real life, if people seem unwilling to come to church with me, then I let them go – after I've said my piece. I'm allowed to do that, just like I'm allowed to upload what I want in terms of religious content on Youtube (even if it annoys both the religious and the irreligious). It's covered by freedom of speech. I can tell any person what I believe – any person. They don't necessarily have to like it, but I have the right to say it.

I have the right to start my own church through freedom of religion, and if you don't want to hear it, you have to leave. You can't suppress my freedom to say whatever I want – I'm only telling the truth, anyway. If you're religious but you don't appreciate me going around telling people Jesus is a hermaphrodite because he has paps, you can't stop me. You have to accept that I am being honest with my religious belief, and trying to tell people the facts. It's my church. It's my work. It's my belief.

If I want to block people from my channel because of their un-Christian attitude to understanding the mysteries of God, then I can. I don't take pride in it, I don't take pleasure in it. But it's my church. I'm the one who is telling people how it is from the Bible. Take gay marriage, for instance.

People get up in arms about gay marriage. It's one of the hot button topics in the United States amongst religious people. Because most religious people believe that gay marriage is evil and shouldn't be allowed, I'm sure you'd expect me to be against gay marriage.

I'm not.

Because I know the Bible properly, unlike most people who simply use it as a prop to hide behind their fears.

Jesus loves the homosexuals too. Jesus loves everyone; this is what you have to understand. In 1 John 4:19 it reads "we love him, because he first loved us. If a man say, I love God, and hateth his brother, he is a liar: for he that loveth not his brother whom he hath seen, how can he love God whom he hath not seen? And this commandment have we from him, That he who loveth God love his brother also."

Now if you knew you were gay since you were a child, you have a right to be gay – whether it's your choice or not. You have that right from God. It's a choice, like any choice given to us by Jesus Christ. In the olden times, with Moses, this was forbidden. You weren't allowed to be gay. By grace you can be gay and straight also. You have a choice! You can be gay, straight or celibate – one of the three. Some people are celibate. Some people don't have sex at all. That just means they love the Messiah more than they love another person. That means they're not going to find someone to marry. Marriage can be a mistake, you know. You can marry someone and it not works out. I know that. It's happened to me. Right now, for example, I'm celibate and that's okay. I love Jesus more than I love anyone else. I haven't been with a woman for two years, since my girlfriend Maude. At the same time, Jesus loves everyone. He loves the homosexuals the same as he loves the heterosexuals – and that's the truth.

If you felt that way since you were a child, more power to you. If you want to be gay, be gay. You can be gay as a choice as well. It is a choice. It's a choice because you can choose it, just like you can choose to be straight or celibate. You can choose it willingly. As long as you only marry one person, then you are fulfilling the word of God – so long as you don't commit adultery towards that person.

I'll grant gay people that. They can marry. I think it's an important ability for people. God judges adulterers, not straight or gay people.

If you're with one person, regardless of their sex, you're fulfilling the law of God. It's the same as being married in a straight marriage. You can be married to a homosexual and be with God. I want you know that. Jesus loves us all. Jesus loves the sinners and the saints; he loves the sinners more because those are who he died for.

So long as you adhere to the Ten Commandments – of which the heart is don't commit adultery – then you're obeying all the commandments of God. If you are in a homosexual union, so long as you stay with that person forever, you're honouring God. God will love you too. God can do that. God has the power to forgive even as we are forgiven. We're all sinners saved by grace. No-one is perfect. That's the point.

People in this country, and people who believe in God are often so closed-minded. You have to be open-minded, because that's the point of religion. We're all the same. We all sin. We all do wrong.

Homosexuals need Jesus too. Jesus died for homosexuals' sins as well as mine. He didn't just die for the sins of the straight people, he died for the sins of the straight people as well. Come on people! Get real! These people aren't bad people, they're good people. They get on with everybody, and try to make a life for themselves. Take Elton John. He is a good gay man: you can get along with him. He doesn't try and force other people to be gay with him: it's their choice.

It's your right to be gay or straight. If you say you're gay, Mr. John doesn't try to make you straight. Vice versa. The gays need Jesus too. Everybody needs Jesus Christ for the absolution of their sins. My view is that if you do the right thing, Jesus will do the right thing for you. That's the whole point. All mankind. That's who he died for. Not just for the straights alone: for the gays as well. I spoke out about this when people were afraid to. I made Youtube videos about gay marriage and gay rights. I put my voice out there, because the religion that I practice is inclusive not exclusive.

I'm backed up by the scriptures, too. John 14:6 says "Jesus saith unto him, I am the way, the truth, and the life: no man cometh unto the Father, but by me." Now if this is true, the gay man cometh to the Father by Jesus Christ too. Everyone comes through Jesus Christ. Think of it this way: we're all the children of God. We're united. There is no difference between us: black or white, straight or gay. It's as simple as that.

My message is we need to love each other than we did in the past. In the past we've done each other wrong; we keep doing each other wrong. We're selfish and greedy and only care about ourselves. That's why I upload singing videos: we can bring people together by singing, in perfect harmony. We need to love each other and treat each other right as well as we can, so we can overcome our mistakes. We all make mistakes – that's a given. But we need to overcome them. I'm trying, through uploading videos, to understand that we need to love and tolerate each other, and most importantly, to co-exist with each other.

I'm most proud of a couple of my videos. I like all the videos I upload; it's hard to put one or two above the rest, but I like 'Jack and Diane' by John Mellencamp; I like 'Every Rose Has Its Thorn' by Poison. I think they were my best work, and I think they were amongst the most entertaining. They weren't overly viewed, but it's like choosing a rare B-side from a Beatles album that only got a limited release. The ones that are overlooked are often the best. 'Jack and Diane' only got about 300 views (since I've mentioned it here, I'm hoping it might get a few more). 'Every Rose' only has a hundred or so more views than that. But they're both fun, they're entertaining (I hope) and I had a lot of fun making them.

Truth be told, I think that's the most important piece of advice I can give anyone wanting to make it big on Youtube. You have to have fun yourself. If shows through the camera. People can read your emotions, and they buy into it. They begin to follow you. If they can chart your happiness and your sadness, then they're more likely to follow you. They like to be engaged; they want to be part of your life. That's important if you're a life blogger.

If you're an entertainer, then they want to see that you yourself are entertained by your performance. It doesn't matter if you're the best singer in the world – if you're not having fun, and it's noticeable, then people won't watch your video. No-one wants to see someone singing the Lion King with a frown on their face.

Singing has always been a big part of my life. While I was in the navy I tried song writing to get over the loneliness and the bad time I was having. I tried to channel my more negative moments into something productive. When people were picking on me the most, that's when I wrote my best songs.

I sent off a demo tape to a record company whose details I managed to get hold of. I sent them two self-penned songs: 'Who's to Blame' and 'Something About You'. I never heard anything back. I guess they were busy.

At the same time (about 1993) I also sent off a tape of me singing to a band who had advertised for a lead singer. I did a combination of Led Zeppelin, my own songs, and a couple of different other artists like Prince (because I can harmonize with him on 'When Doves Cry'). I reckon Prince sounds a little like George Cliton. They didn't get back to me either: though my return mailing address was the barracks at the navy, which I never went back to – so maybe they did and I just never knew.

I used to sing to my ex-wife Daphne when we were together. We met at Portsmouth Naval Hospital. I was being discharged at the time for my paranoid schizophrenia, and she was also in the neurology department for a brain tumor she had. We got talking, and things seemed to click. It was like we were placed on this rollercoaster ride which began hurtling along and we couldn't stop. It was fearful and intoxicating.

We hooked up a few hours after we first met, and rushed off to rent a motel room. We locked ourselves in there and had a lot of sex. It was, like I said, a true whirlwind romance. She seemed really interested really quickly in learning all about me and my life story, and took an interest when I told her a few details, so I let her into the secret that I believed I was one of the two witnesses. At the time I didn't tell many people that, because it gave you a stigma.

The pace of the romance kept its breakneck speed: we wound up getting married within a month of seeing each other for the first time. At the time, it seemed like the right thing to do: we were deeply in love, and we wanted to make this big commitment, so we jumped in with both feet. I don't regret it, looking back. It was a good time, and I think we both thought it was meant to be. She also got pregnant pretty much right away, and we were lucky enough to have Jonathan, our son. Me and my son still get along alright today. We haven't seen each other for a while – about a year, as I write this – but we talk on the phone and check that each of us is getting on okay.

Daphne already had a daughter at the time, and at first things didn't seem too bad. But after a couple of months of marriage I began to think that maybe she had an ulterior motive. I felt like she was using me, and chose to marry me, specifically so that she could get her daughter down to Virginia. She wanted her daughter

– who became my step-daughter – to be part of a family, and that was the only way she could move her interstate.

I was getting hugely stressed by her daughter moving in with us. I had a dream one time – and it was only one time, and it was only a dream – that she was sitting on my couch, and I licked her vagina a little and I masturbated. It was only a dream; it was total fiction. The only fiction in my entire life. I told the story on Youtube (which got me into lots of trouble, because some stupid people couldn't realize that I was describing a dream and that it didn't really happen) as a way to highlight the problem of child molestation and the mentally ill, and to point out that pedophilia is an illness.

All I said was that I had dreamt it, yet people took it entirely the wrong way. They seemed unable to parse the words that I used on the Youtube video I uploaded about the dream (which has since been taken down for inciting hate speech): I said "it could have been a dream", which it was, and people took that as me saying that it wasn't a dream but it happened in real life. That's wrong. It didn't happen. It was just a hypothetical – purely hypothetical – example of how to confess something difficult. What happened is I said on one of my blogs that I could have molested my stepdaughter, because of the schizophrenia, though I didn't, and someone took it out of context, and started harassing me about it, so I told two different stories, including the one in the video. It is just an example of what I believe would have been the worst I could have done if the schizophrenia caused me to act that way. I need to be clear: I didn't molest my stepdaughter. However, things got difficult between me and Daphne, because of some totally unrelated stuff.

The day-to-day married life with Daphne was neither bad nor good. It was basically normal. Occasionally we would get into fights – a lot of them caused by the step daughter, who I thought was a big trouble causer who reveled in it, even though people say because she was just four years old she couldn't be – and arguments and all of that, but I never hit her. I never beat her. Just like I never molested her daughter. I had plenty of reasons to hit her, though.

Once she left me in Buck Snort, TN, or somewhere like that. I don't properly remember. But we were there, and she just upped and left. I had to call my mom to wire me some money to get home. That wasn't good. I managed to get a church to put me up in a motel that night, by the grace of God.

The cost of having a wife gave me lots of problems too: I got in trouble with my creditors and defaulted on some bills. I had Radio Shack, Sears and eventually Wachovia and Crescent Banks coming after me for payments.

By six months into the marriage I had had enough. I felt she was screwing me around, and I legally separated from her. I needed a clean break. All that I had hoped for was for naught. I'd still like to meet a good woman one day, maybe get married and settle down. I met someone who I thought was that, and because she was such a big part of my life I involved her in my videos on Youtube.

Molly came down to Georgia to visit me. If you go to one of my old Youtube accounts (I had to keep changing them when I got new computers or when someone complained about one of my videos) called selee1shane then you can see the videos she made and uploaded. At first, she spent a week with me and had a really good time. We went all over the place. We visited the cemetery and saw some graves of my relatives: my dad, and a few others. Molly took some great pictures of me which were really touching.

We had a great time and I enjoyed her company a lot. She was really pretty, and took a big interest in my family and my life. I took her to the Mount Maria Missionary Baptist Church – the church I first went to as a child, and I explained my spirituality to her. She met Myron and got on well with him, which I think is important. Basically I took her all around the highlights of my life: I took her to where I had my car accident, to the Pineora Speedway, where I'd go swimming when I was a kid. I thought it was important to let her know all about me, and about the places that made me who I am. That's why I gave her the grand tour of Georgia.

We saw lots of movies: Hairspray, I Pronounce You Chuck and Larry, and The Simpsons Movie.

It was sweet. It was like we were lovebirds; young awkward kids. We tanned on the beach at Tybee Island, and Molly got burned so I had to put some suntan lotion on her. We were supposed to go on a carriage tour but we forgot, because we were having so much fun. Molly met my mom and my sister and her husband, and my nephew. They all seemed to get along really well. She liked my cat, Kelly. Then that trip ended all too soon. Molly had to go home. I was sad taking her back to the airport, but she promised to come back.

Molly was a real woman. She responded like a woman, not like a transsexual. She didn't need lubrication.

She was sweet. We had fun. She came back another time, for slightly longer – I think it was 8 or 9 days. It made me feel great: we got to know each other a little better, but all too soon she had to leave again. I hoped that she'd come back about Christmastime for her winter vacation. It was the start of a beautiful friendship.

But it wasn't to be. We eventually began getting complacent, and we kept losing touch. She didn't come back. It happens, I guess. I was sad, but a long-distance relationship was going to be hard. She understood me, though. I was glad she understood me.

I used to be thin. Before I joined the military, I was 145lbs. After, I gained weight and started bulking up. Then with my disability, I gained a lot of weight. I'm around 240-250lbs right now. I've tried diets, and nothing seems to work. I tried starving myself. That doesn't even work. I eat less than 2,000 calories a day across two meals. Nothing seems to work. I've tried all supplements and all fads that there are. I took Stacker 2 to help me lose weight before the accident, and it worked really well. When I couldn't exercise, after the accident, and took it, it did nothing. I had a Torso Track 2 as well, which is an exercise machine, and that helped a little bit but didn't really make many inroads into my weight loss.

I'm on a bunch of medication. I'm on potassium chloride. There's some stuff I can't pronounce: forozamine, carvedudividol, lyzinopril, ibuprofen (for my ankle and pelvis), symbistotin (for my cholesterol), aspirin, respiridone 4mg for the schizphrenia and loratadine for allergries. It's a potent combination. There are too many of them. There are so many of them.

These days, getting through the day is hard. I get up anywhere from 8am to midday, depending on how much my back, pelvis and ankle hurt from whatever I've been doing the previous day. Sometimes the pain wakes me up early; sometimes the thought of bearing weight on broken down joints makes it altogether too difficult to get up before lunchtime. I either eat a bowl of cereal or go out to eat. I like a lot of places. You can find me at Carrey Hillard's, Burger King, Krystals, McDonald's, Applebee's or the Morrison's Café. I like eating fried chicken a lot: I guess it's the Southern way. I like the white meat, but I'll also eat the dark. I like it with mashed potatoes and gravy. I like mac and cheese, and hamburger steak and occasionally even push the boat out to have veal.

I walk at least an hour a day – though it's hard with the pain. I walk over a mile; about two miles, really. I just need a lot of help in a lot of areas, and I don't seem to be getting a lot of help. I'm just trying to get my story across, so I can get some help. It's been hard since my dad was shot: I've been through religions and all that, and tried to get a grip on life and do better for myself and others.

I started hearing voices from an early age. It got worse when I got into the military, after the Persian Gulf War started. I became paranoid that it would start up again, and here we are! It did start up again, and I was proved right. I'm not crazy. I'm just trying to get my life together, and help our fellow man.

The fear about the Persian Gulf War I think I can trace back to a couple of things in my childhood. I watched a movie about Vietnam – I don't remember the name, but I remember the vivid memory it instilled in me. It showed people how terrible it was over there, and it scared me as well. It scared me so much that when I joined the military, I chose the navy for several reasons, one of which was that the navy was at sea and so was less likely to be a target. Don't get me wrong: I was joining the navy for the right reasons. I wasn't going to be a shirker. I wanted a branch where I could have a long career. Before I got there and endured the personal attacks, the bullying and the accident, I was prepared to make it my life. That's why I chose to be an electrician. People always need electricians, and the military always needs them. I thought I was set for life.

Another thing that happened – or rather, another thing that I saw – which I think fuelled a lot of my fears was a documentary that I saw when I was young about Nostradamus.

I don't know if you know about Nostradamus, but when I saw this documentary my eyes were opened. I was young and impressionable, and this documentary repeated one of his premonitions that by 1994 we would be deep into World War III, and that the threat of nuclear weapons would be used to defeat the United States in a sneak attack. When I got to the Christian Fellowship Church, I asked the general pastor there about it and he made it worse by saying that it was entirely possible that Nostradamus was right. He said that he thought Russia would get involved in the War in Iraq, and that they could easily use nuclear weapons. Now bear in mind the timeline. This was the early 1990s, and I was part of a military that was getting heavily involved in the First Persian Gulf War. 1994, the year that Nostradamus predicted would throw the world into havoc, was getting close. I was understandably nervous. I looked into Nostradamus' writings a little more, and I was worried by what I found.

Nostradamus spoke of a man who would turn up that he called the antichrist. He said that the antichrist would wear a dark blue turban. Now at the time, the TV news was showing pictures of Saddam Hussein wearing a light blue turban all the time. I was panicked.

People like the atheists, people who don't embrace religion have a reason for it. There might be a good reason, but you can't prove that what we believe was a myth. We have evidence of his existence through Roman and Jewish historians. It's not like we're making all this up.

Colds and little things like that seem to affect me lots. Sometimes I'm tired. Sometimes I can't sing.

There's proof for religion and evolution. It's things like that which sort of throw people off. Creation and evolution have evidence to back them up. Hummingbirds are perfect: the beak is just as long as the flower they get their nectar from. There are two ways you can look at it: either the hummingbird was created to have his beak that long because God knew it would need it to be that long to get to the nectar, or it evolved that way. The choice is yours as to what happened. I don't know. Maybe it's a bit of both. Maybe it evolved that way because it didn't have any other way to feed. I don't know. We've got to bridge the gap. We've got to come to a meeting of minds, and come to an understanding that we all need to learn to get along despite our differences and help people who have faith, and help those who don't have faith either.

You need to be empathetic with people around you; you need to share the same thoughts, feelings, ideas, motives and situation with them. You do that already, pretty much. We all grow up in similar circumstances. God put us on this planet, and he put everything we would need with us, and knows every possible combination that we can come up with. Let people express themselves how they want; let them think what they want. But teach them right from wrong. You have to do that.

We're to help each other out because we're all human beings. If there's a God, he's waiting in heaven to return for some reason. When he comes back, what's he going to do other than establish his kingdom, and set up rulers, and go away again. He ain't going to stick around to sort us out. We need to learn how to grow up and be adults and do things on our own and get along with people. That's what I want from this world. That's my aim.

Here's hoping that we all learn to get along together.

SHANE EDWARD LEE

E

Effingham, 47, 51
Egypt, 75
Ellen Degeneres, 10
Elton John, 214
Encyclopedia Dramatica, 195
Evil Knivel, 22

F

Faggots, 195
fire, 13, 22, 73
Florida
  Orlando, 29, 30
Fox News, 207, 208

G

gay, 34, 46, 47, 70, 150, 212, 213, 214, 215
GED, 57, 64, 66, 201
Georgia
  Forsyth, 56
  Garden City, 26, 51, 63, 171, 173, 183, 203
  Guyton, 58
  Pineora, 56, 220
  Savannah, 2, 3, 18, 21, 26, 62, 65, 67, 148, 153, 171, 176
  Skidaway, 26
  Statesboro, 56
  Tybee Island, 2, 20
Glenn Beck, 207, 209, 211
God, 3, 6, 8, 9, 10, 11, 15, 24, 26, 39, 40, 45, 46, 58, 59, 60, 62, 67, 68, 69, 70, 72, 75, 76, 141, 145, 146, 147, 150, 151, 152, 154, 157, 160, 163, 166, 167, 168, 170, 171, 172,

179, 183, 186, 187, 188, 190, 191, 192, 193, 194, 209, 211, 212, 213, 214, 215, 219, 224, 225
Granddaddy Lanky, 19
Gulf War, 49, 70, 222, 223

H

Harry Potter, 4
Holy Land, 76
Holy Trinity, 69
hospital, 14, 59, 60, 62, 140, 141, 144, 163, 175, 180, 199
Hot Wheels, 22, 24
Humpty Dumpty, 140
Hurricane David, 37

I

injuries, 140, 142, 143, 164, 178, 183
internet, 9, 166, 172, 185, 186, 187, 194, 195, 196, 204, 205, 211
Iraq, 223

J

James Dean, 57
Jay Leno, 10
Jean-Jacques Rousseau, 165
Jehovah's Witnesses, 67, 68
Jerusalem, 72, 75
Jesus Christ, 1, 3, 8, 39, 41, 46, 67, 75, 76, 140, 141, 142, 146, 149, 160, 161, 162, 167, 188, 212, 213, 214, 215
Jewish, 69, 224
Jimmy Kimmel, 9
Jonathan Rowen Sebastian Lee, 181
Joseph of Arimathea, 1

Judas, 150
judgment, 143, 150
Judgment, 3

K

Kabala, 73
Kama Sutra, 147
karate, 52, 53, 54, 55, 60, 141, 147,
    169, 201
KFC, 183
Ku Klux Klan, 25

L

Lady Gaga, 31
lap dance, 149
Led Zeppelin, 216
lie, 26, 43, 44, 60, 150
Lisa, 46, 56, 75, 149
Little Bobbie, 29
Little Caesar's Pizza, 176
Little Roddy, 28, 52, 57, 60, 61, 156
Lucifer, 150

M

Malcolm Gladwell, 189
Maribel, 147, 148, 151
marijuana, 12, 14
Mark, 28, 168, 169, 170
Mary Magdalene, 1
masturbation, 41, 45, 46, 48, 147, 152
McDonalds, 64
Mecca, 30
medication, 49, 199, 200, 221
Melissa Joan-Hart, 179
memory, 1, 7, 15, 25, 57, 62, 71, 163,
    165, 223

molest, 190, 195, 218
Molly, 219, 220
mom, 1, 3, 4, 5, 6, 7, 8, 11, 12, 14, 20,
    21, 22, 23, 24, 26, 27, 28, 29, 61,
    62, 64, 148, 165, 171, 219
Montel Williams, 10
Mosheh, 46
Mount Carmel, 167
murder, 38
Myra, 29
Myron, 32, 39, 55, 56, 153

N

navy, 47, 49, 63, 64, 65, 66, 67, 68, 69,
    70, 72, 73, 74, 75, 77, 82, 141, 142,
    144, 146, 147, 148, 149, 155, 169,
    172, 173, 175, 176, 178, 179, 180,
    181, 186, 198, 199, 200, 201, 204,
    205, 216, 223
near-death experience
    30-foot fall in navy, 79
    car crash, 57
    drowning, 21, 30
    Jawbreaker indicent, 4, 5, 6, 7, 57
nigger, 25
ninja, 55, 169
Nostradamus, 223, 224

O

Oprah Winfrey, 10
Ozzy Osbourne, 12

P

paper, 2, 17, 18, 39, 165, 186, 188
paps, 160, 212
pelvis, 140, 141, 142, 143, 178, 222

W

Wall Street, 18
Walmart, 18
Wayne's World 2, 191
White House, 13
Wikipedia, 195
Wood Packing Company, 65, 172
World War II, 66

World War III, 223

Y

Yahtzee, 13
Youtube, 9, 10, 24, 30, 55, 162, 164,
187, 188, 191, 192, 193, 194, 195,
196, 204, 207, 208, 209, 210, 211,
212, 215, 216, 218, 219